Helen Ba...

CROSSFIF

by Michel Azam

Translated by Nigel G ...y

A Paines Plough Programme/Text

This publication was made possible with the support of the
Cultural Department of the French Embassy, London

OBERON BOOKS • LONDON • ENGLAND

First published in English 1993 by Oberon Books Limited
521 Caledonian Road
London N7 9RH
Tel: 071 607 3637
Fax: 071 607 3629

ISBN 1 870259 34 3

Printed by The Longdunn Press, Bristol
Cover design by Andrzej Klimowski

OBERON BOOKS LTD
Publisher: James Hogan
Managing Director: Charles Glanville
Associate Editor: Nicholas Dromgoole MA [Oxon] FIChor
Design Consultant: Andrzej Klimowski

NEW THEATRE NEW WRITING

Paines Plough is Britain's leading touring company specialising in new theatre by new writers. Over its nearly twenty year history, the company has established an enviable reputation for its high standards of production and performance. Since it was founded in 1974, the company has been constantly developing and expanding its mission to bring the highest standard of contemporary theatre to the widest audience possible - touring productions both nationally and internationally.

Paines Plough passionately devotes itself to seeking the fresh, the vigorous and the immediate. It is committed to writing as part of a total theatre; musicians and dancers, as well as actors, designer and director work together with the writer towards the most consciously theatrical results.

In addition to mounting the best new plays, the company is unique in that it works nationally with writers at all stages of development. We receive and respond to hundreds of scripts each year. We commission plays and provide Workshops for writers as well as Laboratories and public Rehearsed Readings. As a writers' company with a prolific track record of producing and developing new writing, **Paines Plough** recognises that its role and responsibility must lie in identifying, encouraging and promoting tomorrow's theatre.

"fresh-minted theatrical language...spine-tingling"
THE TIMES

institut français

17 Queensberry Place London SW7 2DT. Telephone: 071-589 6211
Fax: 071-581 5127

The Institut Français offers a wide variety of activities including theatre, talks, exhibitions, cinema, concerts and opera.

Our facilities include a 350-seat theatre, the biggest French library in the UK with 85,000 books, as well as a video club.

We are the official French government centre for language and culture in London and offer a unique choice of courses together with a wide range of days, times and levels to suit your needs.

The Institut Français hosts a number of seminars and conferences throughout the year in collaboration with British higher education institutions.

Members of the Institut Français receive special benefits including free tickets for the Cine Club and free use of the library. Please contact the Membership Office for further information.

French culture, with a London address

Paines Plough presents
the UK Premiere of

CROSSFIRE

by Michel Azama
Translated by Nigel Gearing

Yonathan, 15
Dead Man Covered in Mud   **Silas Carson**

Krim, 17
Dead Man Covered in Seaweed
Renaud the Woodcutter   **Darrell D'Silva**

Ismail, 15
Little Boy   **George Eggay**

Mother Hen   **Stephanie Fayerman**

Old Woman   **Celia Hewitt**

Bella, 20
Little Girl   **Shona Morris**

Old Man   **George Parsons**

Zack, 35
Dead Man Blackened by Smoke
Passerby   **Nigel Whitmey**

Directed by	**Anna Furse**
Designed by	**Sally Jacobs**
Music and Sound by	**Stephen Warbeck**
Lighting by	**Jenny Kagan**
Assistant Director	**Shabnam Shabazi**
Production and Company Manager	**Simon Brophy**
Deputy Stage Manager	**Clare McCaffrey**
Assistant Stage Manager	**Ruth Patchett**
Wardrobe Supervisor	**Ruth Walker**

First performance at The Traverse Theatre, Edinburgh August 24, 1993
Presented in London in association with Soho Theatre Company at the Cockpit

BIOGRAPHIES

SILAS CARSON Trained at the Drama Centre, London. Theatre credits include *The Assassin, Creditors* and *The Lover* (Pentagon Theatre Co.), *Noel Coward in Two Keys* (Thorndike Leatherhead and national tour), *Wuthering Heights* (Theatre Royal York), *Twelfth Night* (Peter Hall Co.), *Romeo and Juliet* and *Taming of the Shrew* (Royal Lyceum, Edinburgh), *Unidentified Human Remains* (Traverse Theatre and Hampstead Theatre) and *Heer Ranjha* (Tara Arts). Television credits include *The Golden Years* and *Horse Opera*.

DARRELL D'SILVA Worked in Sheffield for six years with various bands, and sound and vision projects. Trained at the Drama Centre, London where his credits included Pertinax Surly in *The Alchemist*, Edward Broderick in *South* directed by Anna Furse, Bernardo in *West Side Story*, Ralph Nickleby in *Nicholas Nickleby* and Lear in *King Lear*. Darrell was selected for the BBC Radio Carleton Hobbs Award 1993.

GEORGE EGGAY Trained at the Drama Centre, London where his credits included Drugger in *The Alchemist*, Belling in *An Enemy of the People*, Uncle John in *South* directed by Anna Furse, Tony in *West Side Story*, and Mr. May in *Paradise Lost* directed by Colin Gray. Television credits include *Between the Lines: Crack Up* for the BBC.

STEPHANIE FAYERMAN Theatre includes seasons at Sheffield Crucible, Liverpool Everyman and Liverpool Playhouse. Credits include *Taming of the Shrew, The Crucible, Miss Julie, Roots*, and 'Donna' in Ron Hutchinson's *Says I Says He* directed by David Leland, (Sheffield and the Royal Court). Other theatre includes *Self Portrait* (Derby Playhouse), *What Every Woman Knows* and the title role in *Prin* (West Yorkshire Playhouse). London theatre includes *Marie and Bruce* (Royal Court Theatre, Upstairs), *Ten Times Table* (The Globe), *These Men* (Bush Theatre), Ilona in *The Power of the Dog, The Cartheginians* (Hampstead Theatre), and *The Europeans* (Greenwich Theatre and tour). Credits for the RSC include *Tartuffe, The Roaring Girl, The Taming of the Shrew* and *Maydays*. Television includes 'Aggie' in *Backs to the Land, The Sandbaggers, Agony*, 'Donna' in *Bull Week*, 'The Editor' in *A Very British Coup*, and 'Gwen' in *All Good Things*.

CELIA HEWITT grew up in Norfolk, London and North Wales. Graduated BA Honours in French and Spanish from the University of London. Worked in repertory theatres all over England and Wales including the Theatre in the Round, Scarborough, Halifax, Guildford, Windsor and Colwyn Bay. During seasons at the Duke's Playhouse Lancaster, the Everyman Liverpool and the Stables Theatre Manchester, Celia played Mrs. Loman in *Death of a Salesmen*, Mrs.

Lovett in *Sweeney Todd*, Helen in *A Taste of Honey*, Dunyasha in *The Cherry Orchard* and Mrs. Bryant in *Roots*. Celia toured with 7:84 playing the Mother in *Trafford Tanzi*, and played Mistress Quickly in *Henry V* at Ludlow. Celia has appeared in six films and many TV plays and series. She runs Ripping Yarns, a secondhand bookshop in Highgate specialising in children's books, and is on the committee of Medical Aid to Iraq.

SHONA MORRIS Trained at Jacques Lecoq School of Mime, Movement and Theatre, Paris. Recent theatre includes Hope in *Beat the Air* (Finborough Arms), Lisbeth in *The Hour of the Lynx* (Inner City), Blanch Ingram in *Jane Eyre* (Sheffield Crucible), Annie Hines in *A Better Day* (Stratford East). For Paines Plough she created the title role in the Time Out Award winner *Augustine (Big Hysteria)* (British and Russian tour). At the Royal National Theatre her credits include *School for Wives*, *Yerma* and Masha in *The Mother*. Other theatre includes Martha in *The Nest* (York), Bianca in *The Taming of the Shrew* (Stratford East), Miranda in *The Tempest* (Kick Theatre), *The Bacchae* (Shared Experience), and *Say Your Prayers* (Joint Stock). Seasons at Manchester Contact, Sheffield, Oxford Playhouse, Westcliff and Leicester. Recent television includes *The Buddha of Suburbia*, and *Early Travellers in North America*. Film credits include *Tess*, *Memoir to the Future*, *Little Dorritt*, and *Shredni Vashtar*. Radio includes *Little Dorritt*. Shona has just returned from working at the Comedie de Caen in a bilingual workshop organised by Paines Plough.

GEORGE PARSONS has played a great variety of roles, including in repertory, Trofimov in *The Cherry Orchard*, Mazzini Dunn in *Heartbreak House*, The Gentleman Caller in *The Glass Menagerie*, Tom in *The Norman Conquests*, Face in *The Alchemist*, Ben in *The Dumb Waiter*, Wang in *The Good Woman of Setzuan*, Lieut-Cmdr Bill Rogers in *French Without Tears*, George in *Jumpers*, The Dauphin in *Saint Joan*, and Vladimir in *Waiting for Godot*; in London, Farmer Shiner in an adaptation by Patrick Garland of *Under The Greenwood Tree* (Vaudeville), Dr. Syringe and the Periwigmaker in Vanbrugh's *The Relapse* (Old Vic), Inspector Bridewell in Feydeau's *No Flies On Mr. Hunter* (Chelsea Centre), and Paddy in Paines Plough's *Down and Out in Paris and London* (Riverside Studios); and with the Royal Shakespeare Company, Bloody Serjeant and Doctor in *Macbeth*, Agrippa in *Antony & Cleopatra*, Friar Francis in *Much Ado About Nothing*, Ligniere in *Cyrano de Bergerac*, and Gentleman Starkey in *Peter Pan*. On television he has been seen in *Z-Cars, Crown Court, Together, The Lady Killers, Moliere* and *Cyrano de Bergerac*. He has twice been a member of the BBC Radio Drama Company with whom he has broadcast performances in scores of plays. He wrote *An Empty Glass*, which was performed on BBC radio.

NIGEL WHITMEY Trained at RADA. Theatre work includes *The Revenger's Tragedy* (Cambridge Theatre Company), *Disneyland It Ain't* (Royal Court), *Hell's Kitchen* (Lancaster Dukes), and View *from the Bridge* (Cheltenham Everyman). Television credits include Sammy Hogarth in *Ruth Rendell's Murder Mysteries*, George Caffyn in *Jeeves and Wooster*, Winston in *Lost Language of Cranes*, Louis in *Streetwise*, *Poirot*, *The Josie Lawrence Show* and *The Paul Merton Show*. Film credits include *Shining Through*.

ANNA FURSE Trained at the Royal Ballet School, Bristol, London and Paris Universities. During the '70s she worked as an Assistant/Translator with Peter Brook in Paris, in Grotowski's 'Paratheatre' experiments and as a writer and performer in the emergent New Dance movement. Productions she has directed (touring the UK, Europe, Asia, the former USSR and the USA) include: (as Artistic Director of Bloodgroup), *Barricade of Flowers*, *Dirt*, *Cold Wars*, *Nature*, *Stroke of Genius*, *Clam*, as well as *Pax* by Deborah Levy for The Women's Theatre Group, *Burns* by Edward Bond (New Midlands Dance), *The Dead* by Anne Caulfield (Old Red Lion), *Job Rocking* by Benjamin Zephaniah (Riverside Studios), *Stand Up* with Jack Klaff (Edinburgh Festival), *A Private View* by Tasha Fairbanks (Graeae), *La Folie* by Cindy Oswin (Scarlet Harlets), *On the Verge* by Eric Overmeyer (Birmingham Rep), *Find Me* by Olwen Wymark (Drama Studio), *Medea* by Euripides (Central School), *South* by Julien Green (Drama Centre) and *Skywoman Falling* by Toby Armour (Traverse Theatre). Productions with Paines Plough include *The Clink* by Stephen Jeffreys, *Feasting on Air* by Suzy Gilmour, *Augustine (Big Hysteria)* which she also wrote, *Down and Out in Paris and London* adapted by Nigel Gearing and *Scenic Flights* by Cindy Oswin. Anna also has extensive experience as a lecturer in numerous colleges and drama schools. *Augustine (Big Hysteria)* won her a Time Out Award for Direction and Writing, and a nomination for the London Weekend Television Plays on Stage Award 1991. She is currently working on a film adaptation of the play for Arena Films.

NIGEL GEARING Previous English adaptations include Molière's *Don Juan* (ATC), Jorge Diaz's *My Song is Free* (Monstrous Regiment). Other writing for the theatre includes: *Snap* (Foco Novo), *Berlin Days Hollywood Nights* (Paines Plough), *The Queen of Spades* (Derby Playhouse), *High Wire* (Husets Theatre, Copenhagen), *George Orwell's Down and Out in Paris and London* (Paines Plough). Film includes scenario of *Ascendancy*, Winner of Golden Bear (Best Film, Berlin Film Festival). Radio includes *Gridlock*, *The Distinguished Thing*, *A Summer Affair* (after Klima), and *Tono-Bungay* (after H.G.Wells).

SALLY JACOBS Designed many of Peter Brook's RSC productions, and has also been involved with his Paris Centre. She lived in the USA for fifteen years, designing and directing in Los Angeles and New York. Since returning to live in London she has designed *Die Fleidermaus* for the Paris Opera, *Turandot* and *Fidelio* for the Royal Opera, and *Eugene Onegin* for English National Opera. She designed *Three Birds Alighting on a Field* and *Hush* for the Royal Court, and for Paines Plough, with whom she is an Associate Artist, *The Clink*, *Augustine (Big Hysteria)*, and *Down and Out in Paris and London*, all directed by Anna Furse. Sally has also directed a new opera by Peter Weingold, *Last Tango on the North Circular*; as well as *The War in Heaven* by Joseph Chaikin and Sam Shepard; and is currently preparing *The Dancing Room* for presentation in 1994.

STEPHEN WARBECK Stephen's composition for theatre includes *Blood, Greenland, Bloody Poetry, A Lie of the Mind, Built on Sand* (Royal Court), *Figaro Gets Divorced, Pioneers in Ingolstadt, Damned for Despair, Judgment Day* (Gate, Notting Hill). Other scores include *The Resistible Rise of Arturo Ui, The Caucasian Chalk Circle* and *The Good Person of Szetchuan*. At the National Theatre, four productions including *At Our Table* and *An Inspector Calls*. His TV work includes *Prime Suspect, You Me and Marley, In The Border Country, Nona, The Changeling, Roots,* and *Bitter Harvest*. With Paines Plough Stephen composed the music for *The Clink*, and *Down and Out in Paris and London*. Stephen also writes and performs with his band hKIPPERS.

JENNY KAGAN Jenny was born in Yorkshire and gained an Honours Degree in Theatre Arts from Leeds University. Jenny has been associated with the Bush Theatre, Half Moon YPT, Gloria Theatre, Wakefield Opera House, Pilot Theatre, Pocket Theatre Cumbria, the Drill Hall Arts Centre and the Comedy Store. Jenny's lighting credits include: *The Old Country* for the Palace Theatre Watford, *The Coaldust Affair* for ATC and *Playing the Wife* for Compass Theatre. *Hecuba* (Gate Theatre), *Phoenix* (Bush Theatre), *The Small Moments in Life* (Festival Hall), *The Man Outside* (Chelsea Centre Theatre), *Between the Lines* (Etcetera Theatre), *The Room* and *Hayfever* (Embassy Studio), *Smouldering Globules of Love* (Edinburgh Festival), *Alice in Wonderland* (Italian Tour), *At Home with the Hardy's* (Lyric Theatre Hammersmith), *Tess* (British Tour), *News Revue* (Tour) and *Not Enough Oxygen* (NTC Theatre NSDF).

Production photographs by Hugo Glendinning. Photo of Azama by Philippe Perrin. Set built and constructed by NLD. With special thanks to Solange Oswald, Anna Cutler, Shaw Theatre Workshop and Stuart Hall - Electric Guitar. Music and sound recorded by Steve Parr at Hear No Evil.

CROSSFIRE

"Intersecting lines of fire produced by having guns, rifles, machine-guns, etc. pointed inwards towards the target from two or more positions"

(As enacted in the Houses of Parliament)

Breckman and Company
Chartered Accountants
49 South Molton Street
London W1Y 1HE

MICHEL AZAMA graduated from the University Paul Valery in Montpelier with a degree in Modern Literature. After training as an actor with René Simon at the Jacques Lecoq School, he became the dramaturg of the Centre Dramatique National/Nouveau Théâtre de Bourgogne in Dijon. He is now the Literary Advisor at the Centre National des Écritures Contemporaines at La Chartreuse in Avignon. His plays include *Bled* (Festival de l'Acte, Metz 1984), *Vie et Mort de Pier Paolo Pasolini* (Paris 1984, London 1986, Brazil 1987, Argentina 1988), *Le Sas* (Theatre des Pays du Nord, Bethune, Théâtre Marie Stuart, Paris 1989, Aix 1992, Lyon 1993, Nimes 1993), *Croisades/Crossfire* (Nouveau Théâtre de Bourgogne, Dijon 1989, Staatstheater de Mayence, Germany 1990, Switzerland 1991, and Paines Plough's Edinburgh, London and UK tour 1993), *Iphigénie ou le Péché des Dieux* (Théâtre en Mai, Dijon 1991), *Azteques* (Nouveau Théâtre de Bourgogne 1992). His work for radio includes *Le Sas* (France Culture 1988, Radio-Sarrebruck 1989, Radio Suisse Romande 1990), *Vie et Mort de Pier Pasolini* (Radio Sarrebruck 1990, Radio Suisse Romande 1990, BBC London 1991). His work for television includes *Le Sas* (Création sur FR3 Lille 1990). As a translator Michel has worked on two Spanish plays: *Elsa Schneider* by Sergi Beibel, and *Naufragios* by José Sanchis Sinisterra.

"We have to hail a great author of epic theatre"
Irena Sadowska Guillon FRANCE CULTURE

Believe me when the war was over we were upset.
War is beautiful. Although it's only beautiful for those who make war.
There's no parallel for war, whether it lasts fifteen years or a hundred it's the
same. The sound of gunfire, the sound of bombings and large shells.
All these noises form a kind of melody, which rocks us to sleep.
Now that we can't hear the bombs anymore, we can't fall asleep.
We are trying to sleep with silence and it is taking us some time.

Teenage boy from the Lebanon, being interviewed in 1992 about the war and ceasefire. [From Childhood Lost - IBW Productions Ltd]

Crossfire is a story of war atrocity. Stories would be more accurate, for it is a text which fearlessly interweaves time, place and generations in a language which leaps from poetic monologues of classic scope to sparse and quotidian dialogues. **Crossfire** might belong to the Brechtian rather than the Aristotelian tradition, but it responds with a non-didactic and lyrical voice to the issues of war, conflict and ethnic division. **Crossfire** is epic in its narrative techniques, yet Azama refuses either to tell a complete story or to employ any of the heroics that even Brecht could not avoid.

If we examine **Crossfire** and ask ourselves "Who is the protagonist, and where are the goodies and baddies?", we discover that we are robbed of such obvious moral guidelines. Instead we are given vibrant portraits: totemic archetypes such as Mother Hen, a couple of elderly Angels, a US mercenary, a bunch of war-polluted teenagers, all of whom collide in the play's catastrophic landscape. As to the location? The author suggests - "a war zone...a checkpoint between the world of the living and the dead, ruins which could equally be those of Sodom and Gomorrah or of Hiroshima". What are we left with then? A terrifying and timeless human drama, a theatre-poem, all at once tender and outraged, violent and impassioned.

Azama, avoiding both sentimentality or platitudes, urges his audience to push through the barriers of what the Americans baldly term 'compassion fatigue', to look deep within ourselves. His theatre suggests in a truly contemporary voice what Artaud sought in his Theatre of Cruelty:

"We are not free and the sky can still fall on our heads.... theatre is made to teach us this" (from *The Theatre and its Double*)

(Anna Furse)

It's the baroque which dominated my writing of the play. A central image of our time might be zapping; zapping is a baroque activity. Theatre cannot change anything. May it long continue to interrogate a few consciences.

(Michel Azama)

PAINES PLOUGH
INTERCHANGE STUDIOS
DALBY STREET
LONDON NW5 3NQ
Telephone 071 284 4483
Fax 071 284 4506

Registered Charity 267523

Paines Plough is celebrating! 1994-95 is our Twentieth Anniversary Season. In an extraordinary period of activity we will be presenting three outstanding co-productions with Salisbury Playhouse: **HOUSE**, a site-specific work devised by Geraldine Pilgrim; **WILD THINGS**, a new play commissioned from Anna Reynolds, a sharp black comedy about the struggle to find true freedom and love in a psychiatric hospital; and **TYGER 2**, a jazz musical by Adrian Mitchell and Mike Westbrook celebrating the life of William Blake, a vindication of the power of poetry, vision and imagination; with **WAX** following later in the season, a new play commissioned for the company from Lavinia Murray exploring the life of Madame Tussauds. **Don't miss out! To learn more about the company and our anniversary celebrations please phone us on 071 284 4483 or write to the address above.**

Soho theatre company at the cockpit

SOHO THEATRE COMPANY was founded in 1969 by Verity Bargate and Fred Proud as a theatre committed to the production and encouragement of new plays. In 1972 the Soho Theatre moved into a tiny basement off Oxford Street, becoming the Soho Poly and launching into a series of fortnightly lunchtime productions.

Throughout the 70's and 80's many hundreds of new writers, directors and actors were given early opportunities at the Theatre and the Soho Poly's reputation was firmly established with premieres form writers including Caryl Churchill, David Edgar, Pam Gems, Barrie Keeffe, Hanif Kureishi, Tony Marchant, Sue Townsend and Timberlake Wertenbaker.

But as atmospheric as the Soho Poly could be, the scale of the cramped basement became more and more prohibitive – not only when it came to employing actors of more than 6 feet, but in trying to meet ever–rising costs with a seating capacity of just fifty.

In September 1992 Soho Theatre Company re–opened in its new home, the Cockpit Theatre – a fully–flexible 240 seat auditorium with studio, rehearsal and office space, a large workshop and a stylishly refurbished bar.

TODAY the Company remains as committed as ever to the production and encouragement of new plays. Under the new artistic direction of Abigail Morris, Soho Theatre at the Cockpit has followed a bold programming policy, mounting premiere productions from **new** writers and hosting work from such companies as Shared Experience, Black Theatre Co–op and Liverpool Playhouse.

Uniquely amongst new writing theatres, we also run an extensive development programme where writers' nights, workshops, rehearsed readings and showcase productions provide writers with a framework within which to develop their craft.

But this level of support is expensive and, beyond the valued funding from the Arts Council and Westminster City Council, we have to raise a further £20,000 every year.

We are indebted to the many companies, trusts and individuals who have so generously supported this work. If you would like to join them, or would like more information on Soho Theatre Company, please call **Mark Godfrey** on **071–262 7907** or write to **Soho Theatre Company, Cockpit Theatre, Gateforth Street, London NW8 8EH.**

CROSSFIRE

No se puede mirar.
Yo lo vì.

It can't be looked at.
I've seen it.

GOYA

CHARACTERS

Young girl
Young boy
Little old man
Little old woman
Mother Hen
Man
Ismail, 15
Yonathan, 15
Krim, 17
An American Indian
Old lady with bucket
Bella, 20
Smoke-blackened man
Zack, 35
Passerby
Dead man covered in mud
Dead man covered in seaweed and kerosene

PROLOGUE

The YOUNG BOY and the YOUNG GIRL are in an empty space, darkness all around.

GIRL

Rrrr-iiii-pppp! [*She pulls an arm off her doll*] My doll's lost an arm in the bombing.

BOY

Quick! You have to burn the wound so it won't bleed.

GIRL

Silly! It's a doll. Dolls don't bleed.

BOY

You have to burn them all the same. You do it like this. [*He cauterises the doll's shoulder with a match*] It stinks. Plastic stinks just like people do when you burn them.

GIRL

My doll's a nice doll. Careful! She was hit by shrapnel. Rrrr-iiii-pppp! Rrrr-iiii-pppp! A leg and now her other arm!

BOY

Stop it. You'll end up killing her.

GIRL

Burn! Go on - burn! Oh, what a brilliant stink! You can get rid of everything - she won't die as long as it's not the head.

BOY

Maybe, but --

GIRL

But once you get rid of the head she dies. Oh! ... Look!

[*A tiny parachute falls from the flies*]

BOY

What's is it?

GIRL

Looks like a present! A treat!

BOY

It's mine!

GIRL

No. It's mine.

BOTH [*Fighting over the package*]

's mine. 's mine.

BOY

I'm stronger than you.

GIRL

You're silly. Silly like all boys. I bet there isn't anything any good in that present. Medicine and rubbish like that.

BOY

You're jealous.

GIRL

No I'm not.

BOY

Yes you are.

GIRL

No I'm not.

BOY

Yes you are. Good. So if you're not jealous why are you crying? Shall I open it?

GIRL

I don't care. I'm looking after my doll or else she'll turn all black like my cousin did when he lost his arm.

BOY

Look. It's a truck. A petrol truck. Oh! It's got a remote!

GIRL

I don't care. It's silly. It's a boys' toy.

BOY

Listen. Don't be cross. Look. I put the truck down here. Right here next to me. And I give you this to steer it with. You press this button - right? - and the truck will come towards you. Okay? You're not still cross, are you? Will you play with me?

GIRL

Good. Yes. Give it here.

[*The BOY is several yards from the GIRL. She presses the remote control button. The truck explodes. The boy turns a somersault and falls lifeless to the ground*]

GIRL

What are you doing? Hey, isn't it a good toy? Hey, what is this toy?

Hey, you're not dead are you?

[*She comes up to the boy*]

He's dead!

Like my cousin, like my aunt, like my uncle, like my father and my little brother
and my uncle Jeremiah.

[*To her doll*]

It's all your fault, you bitch! It's 'cos we got all cross with each other all because of
you. Bitch! Here! This is what happens to dolls like you. One day they're not
paying attention so they tread on a land-mine and whoosh! their head flies off
over the rooftops.

[*She pulls the doll's head off and throws it in the air*]

There you are. You're dead. Well done, bitch! My boyfriend's dead, my doll's
dead, they're all really dead except my mother -- and me, I'm really unhappy.

[*She cries. The dead boy sits up and speaks*]

BOY

It's not serious, you know. Not worth crying about. It didn't hurt and I
"departed this world" as Mummy would say. I departed instantly. It's the best
way, they say, so there you are. When I departed I saw a huge light. I realised I'd
just departed.

GIRL

What's it like to "depart"?

BOY

It's good.

GIRL

It's good. Is that all?

BOY

It's better than playing with dolls.

GIRL

Don't you get bored?

BOY

No. There were other departed people waiting for me.

GIRL

I want to depart as well.

BOY

Departing isn't something you make up your mind to do. You depart or you
don't depart, but you don't just decide to.

GIRL

That's not fair. Lend me your truck.

BOY

Forget it. It can only explode once. Listen. It'll be like a little message for my Mummy. When she gets here she'll get a real shock. She'll see me all stiff and nearly black already.

GIRL

You're not stiff and you're not black.

BOY

That's 'cos I'm only just departed and because you see me like you see me, through your eyes. But my Mummy won't see me like you see me.

GIRL

So how will she see you?

BOY

Through her own eyes. She'll see me departed. That'll upset her a bit. She's used to seeing me alive. You need time to get used to it.

GIRL

She's seen others who've departed.

BOY

Yes, but not me.

GIRL

I want to depart as well.

BOY

Don't keep interrupting. I've got better things to do.

GIRL

What things? You've got nothing to do. The dead sleep under the ground and they do nothing all day, not even at night. In fact they don't even sleep. They do nothing at all. They just lie around getting bored in the middle of heaps of roots and old earth.

BOY

What do you know about it?

GIRL

It's what they teach us.

BOY

They teach you bullshit. Because the living have never departed they've got nothing to say about it. Us dead have a job to do, even the young ones like me.

GIRL

What job?

BOY

It's a secret. That's not the point. I'm talking about my Mummy, who'll cry when she sees me. When you see her you'll tell her that I'm doing fine with the other departed. Okay?

GIRL

You're not doing fine because you're departed.

BOY:

You're stupid. You're just a girl. You don't understand anything. I can see I'm wasting my time. I've got better things to do.

[*He lies down and stops moving*]

GIRL

Don't be cross. Why are you going all stiff again? Stop being dead. I don't want you to be departed any more. I'm not playing any more. Listen. Don't be cross. Stop being dead. Stop departing all the time. You're really stupid with your boys' games. I'm cross too and I'm really unhappy.

[*Burst of machine-gun fire. The girl falls dead. She slowly sits up and says*]

GIRL

Oh! I think I've just departed too.

[*She touches the boy who sits up slowly. They look at each other in silence. They take each other's hand and go off upstage. Upstage we see an elderly couple. She has a white parasol. They're both very smart. They hold their arms out to the two children. The children and the elderly couple disappear as if dissolved by the light*]

SEQUENCE 1

MOTHER HEN, the MAN

[A mythic-looking woman enters wearing a long, shapeless dress of no particular period. This is MOTHER HEN. She speaks directly to the audience. This sequence takes place in a space with darkness all around or among the audience]

MOTHER HEN

Tell me

is it still a long way to Jerusalem?

I'm walking walking walking

I've been walking since the year 1212.

My legs can't take it. So tired.

So very tired. My varicose veins have burst. Pus, pus, fountains of pus.

I've already been dead quite a few years now.

Just because I'm dead until I set foot in Jerusalem there's no question of taking things easy, not until I set foot in Jerusalem.

A vow is a vow and being dead's no excuse.

It can't be far

now. What year are we in?

I count the years in clumps of fifty.

What a to-do.

I set off with this flock of innocents

all the country's brats flooding out in every direction

Let's go forth and liberate Jerusalem.

And we sing and we walk. E SUS E ULTREIA E DEUS AIA NOS.

What a din. Children, all of them children, fair-haired, dark-haired, red-heads, curly-heads, kids with straight-hair, kids blind in one eye, kids who limp, thirty thousand of them, that's what they said, thirty thousand, little girls and little boys all setting off for Jerusalem. It's an old story. My memory's going. Comes back in spurts amid the chaos.

We saw this shepherd, this Etienne, this kid fifteen years old the angels talk to.

WAR!LET'S GO TO WAR!WAR TO THE DEATH!

that's what the angels are supposed to have have said to him.

All the little sheep in his flock went down on their knees before him to beg deliverance for Jerusalem.

The Saracens in the Holy City sprawl on the True Cross, they piss and they shit on the Holy Sephulcre. Deliverance. Deliverance. It's in the Bible. So they tell me. I wouldn't know.

I never learned to read.

So the shepherd and the other kids set off. Forward! Carving the pilgrim's staff from the branch of a hazel-nut tree

E SUS E ULTREIA E DEUS AIA NOS

[*She sits. A MAN in rags enters*]

MOTHER HEN

So who are you?

MAN

I'm Renaud the wood-cutter.

Once upon a time I'd fell an oak tree with just a hundred blows of my axe.

I embraced the faith so I'd no longer be a serf.

I set off with the army of Louis de Blois de Champaigne.

The King's commanders-in-chief, his liege-men, his governors, great vassals, feudal overlords and me who was a serf.

It was a wagon-train waving banners, streamers and flags when we set off. I wanted to travel further than just the Blois and the Vendôme, wanted to see other hills, wanted to see if there was anything else in other parts.

MOTHER HEN

You made it to Jerusalem?

MAN

Yes.

MOTHER HEN

Poor boy. You didn't stay there.

MAN

I want to go home.

MOTHER HEN

Back home they've been dead for ages.

What did you do there? Tell me about Jerusalem.

MAN

We pleased God by liberating the Holy Sephulcre. We killed a lot. Killed in the streets gardens courtyards we burned down the synagogue sent heads spinnning over the tops of walls the whole city was drenched in blood we marched through blood

so thick it came up to our horses' bridles

MOTHER HEN

Not how I'd have imagined you get to please God.

MAN

The city had to be liberated.

At night-fall barons and knights washed and changed and walked barefoot in the blood-drenched streets. Weeping tears of joy they would devoutly kiss the places trodden by the feet of Christ. It seemed to us we were entering Paradise.

MOTHER HEN

Not how I'd have imagined Paradise either.

MAN

It seemed to us we saw the body of Jesus there, lying their dead.

During Mass many soldiers continued to purify the city treading on corpses in their thousands smashing the heads of children against rocks. It was a day of great Christian celebration.

In the church of the Holy Sephulcre barons and knights wept with joy amidst the candles and the smoke from the incense. It is said that on hearing the news the Pope died of joy.

MOTHER HEN

The poor man.

What year are we in?

MAN

I don't know.

MOTHER HEN

Tell me

Is it still a long way to Jerusalem?

MAN

I don't know.

MOTHER HEN

At least tell me the way.

MAN

All roads lead there.

[*He exits*]

MOTHER HEN

Well I'll tell you -- *there*'s someone who hasn't learned much in the Celestial City!

So be it. Onwards!

[*She exits*]

[*The scenery appears. It is a war-zone, at a check-point between the world of the living and the dead, ruins which could equally be those of Sodom and Gomorrah or of Hiroshima*]

SEQUENCE 2

ISMAIL. YONATHAN

YONATHAN

Ismail, I'm going. I mean, I'm not just going, I'm leaving you.

ISMAIL

Where to?

YONATHAN

The other side.

ISMAIL

What. To them others?

YONATHAN

Yes.

ISMAIL

Have you gone mad or what?

YONATHAN

My family's a different religion from yours. We settled here before everything blew up like this. Now it's not the same any more. Our place is over there. Opposite.

ISMAIL

With them others?

YONATHAN

We're part of them others.

ISMAIL

It's crazy. You were born here. We've always played soccer together. It's crazy.

YONATHAN

Absolutely.

ISMAIL

No one will hurt you here. You come from round here.

YONATHAN

Who knows. Things have changed so quickly.

ISMAIL

We're trapped. I feel lost. I try and understand what's going on. I listen to the radio. I try and keep up. This war's a war of lies. Everybody's lying. You can't know any more.

YONATHAN

I've got gut trouble. I'm getting nervous and irritable. I'm sleeping very badly. I can't get to sleep.

ISMAIL

You should count the shells.

YONATHAN

That's what I do. It wakes me up. Ismail, I'm off.

ISMAIL

Wait. You can't leave just like that. We'll still see each other.

YONATHAN

Won't be so easy when we're on opposite sides.

ISMAIL

When we were kids the war was just a good excuse for bunking off school. You remember, we used to say: no school today! today's a bombing-day!

You can't go off with them.

We're lions and they're just dogs.

YONATHAN

That's how it is. There's nothing we can do about it.

ISMAIL

You're my mate. My mate. One hundred per cent. I can't think of you as the enemy, it's impossible. I'd get killed for you here and now like a shot ... Like a shot.

You remember you wanted to be a doctor and me an engineer.

On my fifteenth birthday we had a party, a picnic by the sea with some girls.

There haven't been any since.

YONATHAN

There won't be any more, Ismail.

ISMAIL

Yonathan! We said we'd never split up.

YONATHAN

We were kids. The war hadn't started then. Not really. Not like nowadays.

ISMAIL

Remember, that was the day it began.

YONATHAN

What's the point.

ISMAIL

For our picnic we had a barbecue. We danced with the girls. When we got back we didn't understand what that guy was saying. He was saying things are hotting up out there and when we got back ...

YONATHAN

Yes. Usually a bit of a fuss, a bit of a noise then nothing.

I have to go.

Have to be across the line by nightfall.

ISMAIL

I found my mother in tears. She thought I was dead.

YONATHAN

Mine too. You'd flirted with the most beautiful girl. Let's stop this. It's pointless.

ISMAIL

You were jealous.

YONATHAN

That was in peace time. Not the same.

ISMAIL

We've spent our whole lives playing soccer and stealing figs.

YONATHAN

All that's over now.

ISMAIL

You can't leave just like that. Over on the other side with the others. I don't believe you. Shooting at us. Shooting at me perhaps. I can't believe that.

YONATHAN

Whether you believe it or not makes no difference.

I'm sorry we're not the same religion. One day we could have met up again in the same Heaven.

ISMAIL

You haven't a single real feeling in the whole of your body.

YONATHAN

Yes I have.

ISMAIL

What? What feeling? Tell me.

YONATHAN

The feeling that from one side or another everyone's pushing us towards our graves.

ISMAIL

That's no answer. I don't want you to leave.

YONATHAN

I have to. Give us a hug, Ismail.

ISMAIL

No. Piss off.

They hug. Yonathan runs off.

ISMAIL

Yonathaaaaaaaaan.

Come back. Yonathan. Don't go. Over there they're just dogs and we're lions.

Yonathan.

[*Quick blackout*]

SEQUENCE 3

[*MOTHER HEN, followed by an AMERICAN INDIAN, and the SMOKE
BLACKENED MAN*]

MOTHER HEN

They set off just like that. At first just a few of them.
Then in their thousands.
And, poor wretch that I am, I heard their rumbling.
Rushing down hill after hill like an army of rats
nothing to hold them back not threats not locks not prisons not caresses
they climb the ramparts they abandon their animals out grazing in the fields they
hide in the depths of forests they march they march
the avalanche gets bigger
fathers threaten to kill their sons with axes and clubs
mothers claw at their own breasts and faces
but they don't even bother to look
they fan out between the houses armed with crosses candles censers.
As they pass the bells start ringing of their own accord.
Countless numbers of birds of frogs of butterflies accompany them on their way
to the sea
and, poor wretch that I am, I heard their rumbling.
How to protect my fourteen children my ten boys my four girls from this mania
for Jerusalem? I made up a potion from the balls of a hare and the liver of a dove
I wore a string of garlic round my neck I rubbed their loins with holy water while
they slept
woe betide you I told them woe betide all who go to Jerusalem
Barberossa and Lionheart came a cropper
how could defenceless children hope to succeed?
I told them those who came back had eyes still leaking the horrors they'd seen
they speak spewing it out
of axes sword-points spears daggers Baldwin the Mighty staked out under the sun
his wounds pecked at by birds.
The Saracens tear out the hearts of the wounded to eat them
they copulate with their goats they boil their children.
All my stories just made them laugh.
I locked them up my ten boys my four girls
but when they heard that army of kids singing

they went crazy all fourteen of them.
I had nailed up the doors and the windows.
They found incredible strength in their arms
I lay down across the threshold
and in silence my fourteen children stepped over me.
I followed them I shouted: "Cut me up into little pieces first!"
but they heard nothing they didn't turn back
Without a second thought I picked up my biggest cooking-pot
Let's go! Too bad for my old legs!
Since then I've torn up barley and rye when there's been any
I've made soup in secret soup and then more soup
but it's like trying to feed a swarm of hornets
I've been making them soup for centuries now.
The wind of God drives us on.
In men there are two angels the good and the bad.
Is this the good or the bad
how to decide.
So. Now I've lost my gang of kids.
Have you seen a gang of rats blacking the hillside as they pass by?
[*The INDIAN and the SMOKE-BLACKENED MAN have already been on stage a while.
MOTHER HEN sees them*]
            What is it?
            Oh my ...
            I've never seen a red man.
SMOKE-BLACKENED MAN
            He comes from America.
MOTHER HEN
            America?
            What's this "America"?
SMOKE-BLACKENED MAN
            The other side of the ocean.
            The new world.
MOTHER HEN
            New world.
            Listen, I don't know what you're talking about, my man.

SMOKE-BLACKENED MAN

They've discovered another half of the world on the other side of the ocean.

MOTHER HEN

Another half of the world.

SMOKE-BLACKENED MAN

Yes.

MOTHER HEN

Well, well. Then it must be that second half of the world which is making us lose our balance and shaking the earth up till it goes crazy.

Why are you all black?

SMOKE-BLACKENED MAN

It's the smoke. The Inquisition has just burned me.

MOTHER HEN

Inquisition. What is it this thing which burns people?

SMOKE-BLACKENED MAN

A church tribunal.

MOTHER HEN

Ah! You're a heretic.

SMOKE-BLACKENED MAN

No.

MOTHER HEN

You must have done something.

SMOKE-BLACKENED MAN

No.

MOTHER HEN

Theft, adultery, blasphemy ...

You slept with a cardinal's mistress, the ultimate offence.

SMOKE-BLACKENED MAN

No.

MOTHER HEN

There must have been something.

SMOKE-BLACKENED MAN

I don't have a foreskin.

MOTHER HEN

Ah. Do they burn people for that?

SMOKE-BLACKENED MAN

Walking proof.

MOTHER HEN

What dreadful times!

And him?

SMOKE-BLACKENED MAN

The same thing. The Inquisition.

MOTHER HEN

He hasn't got a foreskin either?

SMOKE-BLACKENED MAN

Yes he has.

MOTHER HEN

Well then?

SMOKE-BLACKENED MAN

He has a red skin.

He does not recognise Christ.

MOTHER HEN

Of course. That makes two good reasons.

Where are you going like that?

SMOKE-BLACKENED MAN

Towards the Promised Land.

MOTHER HEN

This land seems to have been promised to a lot of people. You haven't by any chance seen my thirty thousand children go by?

SMOKE-BLACKENED MAN

Thirty thousand?

MOTHER HEN

Yes. Plus fourteen who came out of my own belly ...

SEQUENCE 4
KRIM, ISMAIL

[*KRIM runs in, a Kalashnikov in his hand*]

KRIM

They're coming. They're coming. The army's coming.

They've put a barricade of rocks and tyres across the road.

ISMAIL

They're very excited.

KRIM

They've set fire to the tyres.

ISMAIL

They're shooting. At least three hundred of them. We'll be slaughtered.

KRIM

They're burning the cars.

ISMAIL

They're torching everything.

KRIM

There's so much smoke. It makes your eyes sting.

ISMAIL

What are you doing?

KRIM

Fried alive is one thing but not with a full bladder.

ISMAIL

Look. A sack. It's tied up with string.

KRIM

Don't touch it. It's a bomb.

ISMAIL

It's got a label.

KRIM

Don't touch it. It's a booby-trap.

ISMAIL.

No it's not. Look. It's come undone.

KRIM

Careful. You'll get yourself killed.

ISMAIL.

It's a man's jacket. Yuk.

It's full of blood.

KRIM.

You're mad. Don't touch it.

ISMAIL.

It's got shoulders.

KRIM.

What.

ISMAIL.

In the jacket ... there's shoulders ... something ... well someone.

KRIM.

Leave it. That's enough.

ISMAIL.

No head. No arms. There's the top half of a man in the jacket. An envelope in the pocket. Shall I open it?

KRIM.

You're mad. You've got no idea. They can put a bomb under a little postage-stamp.

ISMAIL.

It's a pay-slip. Made out to ... To the guy who lives next door.

KRIM.

You shouldn't have touched it. What good's it to us.

ISMAIL.

Shit. I've pissed in my pants. I'm soaking.

KRIM.

It's normal.

ISMAIL.

What do you mean it's normal?

KRIM.

It's panic. Come on.

ISMAIL.

What do we do with this sack?

KRIM.

For fuck's sake, it's not our problem. Come on!

[*They grope silently through the ruins. ISMAIL produces a packet of postcards from a smashed-up box*]

ISMAIL.

See that?

"Hotel Phoenicia" – "the swimming-pool" – "the small stadium" – "the yacht-club".

KRIM.

It was a beautiful city once.

ISMAIL.

Yes. You have to be old to have memories here.

KRIM.

That's for sure. You have to be at least thirty.

ISMAIL.

We'll never make it.

[*They laugh*]

Have you ever seen a shop-front? I mean a real one with things in it – like souvenirs, knick-knacks, and a window in front of them, I mean a real whole glass shop-window?

KRIM.

No. 'Course not.

What are we waiting here for?

ISMAIL.

Nothing. We can see everything from here. If you want to play safe look for the highest point.

KRIM.

Why. So you've got further to fall when it all collapses?

[*They laugh*]

ISMAIL.

So no one can take a pot-shot at you from higher up ... You haven't got a fag, have you?

KRIM.

You must be joking. You have to cross town to get a gas-cylinder, so soon you'll have to cross the desert just to get cigarettes ...

ISMAIL.

And look at that. "Panorama of the Great Hotels."

KRIM.

It's great. It was great. It was really great ...

ISMAIL.

Yeh. You see? There were some red buses and some yellow ones.

KRIM.

Why do you think they had them in red?

ISMAIL.

How should I know.

KRIM.

Or yellow.

ISMAIL.

Listen, they were just buses for people.

KRIM.

When they still had people who caught buses.

ISMAIL.

Yes.

What are we doing here? What are we waiting for?

What's going to happen now? I'm hungry.

KRIM.

We're waiting.

ISMAIL.

For what. What are we waiting for?

KRIM.

Anything. Have to be ready for anything, man. Anything can happen from one minute to the next here. The mud can catch fire.

Careful. Don't move. Someone's crossing the street.

ISMAIL.

It's a woman. An old woman.

KRIM.

Man or woman – you gotta watch out.

ISMAIL.

Come off it. She's going to fetch water.

KRIM.

How do you know?

ISMAIL.

She's got a bucket.

KRIM.

You know what they can hide in a bucket. Don't move. Stay down.

ISMAIL.

I'm telling you, she's going to fetch water. It's an old woman.

KRIM.

So what. Old or not old, she can still be dangerous.

ISMAIL.

You're crazy. There's only our lot round here. She's not from the other side.

KRIM.

How do you know?

ISMAIL.

It's impossible. She wouldn't dare. It's too risky.

KRIM.

That's where you're wrong. Ideas. Never trust ideas. They're infiltrating us.

ISMAIL.

What are you doing? You're crazy. What are you doing?

KRIM.

She's turned round. She's spotted us. Sun reflecting off a gun-barrel – that's all it takes.

ISMAIL.

There's no danger. She's not armed. She's a poor old woman who lives round here. Stop.

KRIM.

And in the bucket? A bucket full of grenades can do a lot of damage.

ISMAIL.

Just an old woman going to fetch water.

KRIM.

How do you know?

ISMAIL.

And how do you know?

KRIM.

When you're not sure you're not sure.

[KRIM loads the rifle]

ISMAIL.

Stop. For one thing you can never be sure. Calm down.

Just an old woman going –

KRIM.

– to fetch water. Yes. But when you're not sure you're not sure. And if you wait till you're sure you're dead.

ISMAIL.

You're crazy. Stop I tell you.

KRIM.

We're in a war-zone. She's spying on us.

ISMAIL.

What are you doing. No. Don't shoot. Stop.

[KRIM shoots]

KRIM.

I got her in the leg. Shit. She's screaming.

I'll teach her how to shut up.

ISMAIL.

You mustn't. Stop. She hasn't done anything. She's from round here. Stop. She's going to get water. She's an old woman. Stop. You mustn't. No. Stop.

[KRIM shoots again]

KRIM.

That's it. Got her.

ISMAIL.

Bastard. It's disgusting. She was going to get water.

KRIM.

She's a spy.

ISMAIL.

Liar.

[The old woman falls down dead then stands up again and speaks]

OLD WOMAN WITH THE WATER-BUCKET.

I'm starting to get everything mixed up.

I jump at the least noise but when it comes to good health Thanks be to God I touch wood

Well, here I am bleeding ... Oh my God these days there's no way of quietly going to fetch water.

You wonder what kind of world we're living in.

No more respect for anything.

Everybody sticks their nose in other people's business and everything goes wrong.

Yesterday I even saw some whores who've opened a jam-co-op.

That is, if you can call it jam.

To find vegetables - that is, if you can call them vegetables - you have to go all over town - that is, if you can still call it a town - and even then you only find them on the black market.

But when it comes to black markets it's well and truly a black market. They sell money at ten times its face value.

And in what was once the cathedral I saw an old bloke pulling up the grass between the paving-stones as he recited prayers which didn't even sound Catholic.

What a world we live in.

Everything up in smoke, everything turning red. The smoke is thickening.

Soon everything will explode and finita la commedia.

I'm bleeding - it's so irritating.

It's crazy how many bandages you can get through ...

Thanks be to God that when it comes to good health --

[*In mid-phrase she falls stone dead*]

ISMAIL.

Assassin.

KRIM.

You haven't got the guts to do that.

[*They run off*]

SEQUENCE 5

[*Lights up on the old couple - very old, very smartly dressed - seen at the end of the prologue. She has a white parasol. Her dress and parasol are splattered with blood. Here amidst the rubble they are quite clearly dead and do not move. After some time they open their eyes and speak*]

LITTLE OLD MAN

Just seeing you from behind was enough. Enough for our meeting to be ...

LITTLE OLD WOMAN

Why go over all that again.

LITTLE OLD MAN

That day I had nothing to do. I just wanted to fall in love and I saw you from behind. I told myself too bad if she's ugly. You turned round: you were not ugly. I was already in love with you.

I'd give anything to see Venice again.

LITTLE OLD WOMAN

Venice! You and your memories ...

LITTLE OLD MAN

Venice, New York, Paris ...

LITTLE OLD WOMAN

That's all over and done with. Another world. Why bother saying those names.

LITTLE OLD MAN

The first day you gently washed my hair under the shower and then we went to the zoo. The pumas the tigers the elephants the monkeys.

LITTLE OLD WOMAN

Shut up. What's come over you rabbiting on like this with your memories. It's excruciating.

LITTLE OLD MAN

On the contrary, it's a pleasure. You know I've always loved you. Even now.

LITTLE OLD WOMAN

And words like that, you should ban them too. Instead you could help me work out how it all happened.

LITTLE OLD MAN

We were sitting on the terrace.

LITTLE OLD WOMAN

Yes. A plane appeared, weighed down with freight. A huge droning sound.

LITTLE OLD MAN

It was one of those old planes you don't see any more. A bi-plane.

LITTLE OLD WOMAN

Suddenly we heard poppoppop off behind the building. The plane did a slow turn over the marshes and headed back flying very low.

LITTLE OLD MAN

Yes. There was a series of explosions like paper bags being burst and everything around us caught fire.

LITTLE OLD WOMAN

It was a beautiful August evening, fresh and still sunny ...

LITTLE OLD MAN

It was such a natural way for us to die.

LITTLE OLD WOMAN

Yes. And so ... how shall I put it. So natural, yes. So natural to be cut down on the terrace during a game of `boule' ...

LITTLE OLD MAN

It is a privilege to die peacefully in such troubled times.

What are we doing here?

LITTLE OLD WOMAN

You'll never change. Head in the clouds. We've come here to welcome one of those youngsters.

LITTLE OLD MAN

I don't see anyone.

LITTLE OLD WOMAN

Wait. That's because he isn't dead yet.

LITTLE OLD MAN

You're either on time or you're not. In my day they'd never have allowed us to be late for our own death.

LITTLE OLD WOMAN

Death comes to men as it does to beasts: without their knowing.

LITTLE OLD MAN

In Bahia the Campo Santo is spread out across a wonderful hillside. All on different levels facing the sea. On the highest terraces stand the black and pink marble tombs of the sugar-barons the doctors the nobs the plantation-owners the lords of cocoa and coffee. At the foot of the hill a simple stone covers the bodies of the regular employees and lower still in a sort of ravine full of brushwood the unmarked graves of the black workers. Occasionally these are disturbed. People come to dig up these bones with pick-axes to pile them into wheelbarrows to burn them to powder to cast them to the winds ...

LITTLE OLD WOMAN

So what you're saying is the rich stay put while the poor go off on their travels ...

[*Taking short steps, they stroll off amid the ruins, happily holding hands*]

SEQUENCE 6

ISMAIL, BELLA

[BELLA has a rifle trained on ISMAIL]

BELLA

Watch it. I'm armed. Don't move.

ISMAIL

What do you want?

BELLA

Did *you* shoot the old woman?

ISMAIL

No.

BELLA

Who was it then?

ISMAIL

What's it to you?

BELLA

Answer me.

ISMAIL

I don't know.

BELLA

You're lying. It doesn't matter. She's dead and that's that.

ISMAIL

Did you know her?

BELLA

None of your business.

ISMAIL

Was she your mother?

BELLA

My mother died in a bombing-raid.

ISMAIL

Your grandmother then?

BELLA

My grandmother was gassed to death.

ISMAIL

I'm sorry.

BELLA

Forget it ...

ISMAIL

Put down your rifle. It's heavy.

BELLA

Mind your own business. My father taught me how to shoot when I was four. He came to collect me from the children's playground in an armoured car. He taught me the art of camouflage by threading leaves in my hair and how to make it to the top of a hill without being spotted. I was his heroine.

ISMAIL

Not bad for a girl.

BELLA

Fuck that. What counts is the make of rifle and how quick your reflexes are – that's all.

ISMAIL

I like you.

BELLA

Watch it, mate. We're not here to chat each other up. I've got my rifle on you and don't you forget it.

ISMAIL

I'm not forgetting. You're still beautiful.

BELLA

Maybe. That's not the point.

ISMAIL

So what is the point.

BELLA

That's right – you forget soon enough when it suits you. Who killed the old woman? Your mate? Good. Where is this mate of yours?

ISMAIL

I don't know. He left straight away.

BELLA

Got you! You've just admitted it.

You don't bump off an old lady going to fetch water.

ISMAIL

That's what I said.

BELLA

Oh yeh. "That's what you said." Pull the other one.

ISMAIL

I promise you ...

BELLA

Do me a favour, right? Forget it. You're from the other side. You don't seem like it.

ISMAIL

's not about 'seeming'.

BELLA

You still don't seem like it.

ISMAIL

And you?

BELLA

Any of your business? Okay, what the fuck, if you really want to know when I was just a little kid I was five this fucking city had been won back I kissed the wall I was just a little kid but I can still remember that crowd of people heading up to it. There were whole bunches of thorns growing between the stones in the wall. I was walking along next to a paratrooper I said to him "What are you feeling?" he said: "What do you feel? I feel like I'm coming home after 900 years".

I don't know why I'm telling you all this shit.

ISMAIL

Got to talk. Can't always be fighting.

BELLA

You're a bit of all right too.

ISMAIL

A girl shouldn't say things like that.

BELLA

Fuck off, virgin. No one ever said that to you either?

ISMAIL

We're not here to talk about that kind of thing.

BELLA

Whoever's got the gun decides what kind of talk. And me I'm the gun. How come you wander about unarmed? Did you come out for a picnic or what?

ISMAIL

I'm too young to start fighting.

BELLA

So how old?

ISMAIL

What?

BELLA

You deaf or something? I said: how old?

ISMAIL

Seventeen.

BELLA

Call it fifteen max.

ISMAIL

Just 'cos you've got a gun you think you can insult me.

BELLA

I said fifteen. Since when has that been an insult?

ISMAIL

Just 'cos you're on top.

BELLA

Talk all you like. But if you think that'll make me drop my gun ...

ISMAIL

You've got an unfair advantage.

BELLA

Who said I didn't?

ISMAIL

Then don't use it to get personal, to ask me my age and all that ...

BELLA

Sir is very touchy.

ISMAIL

A prisoner deserves respect.

[*Bella chokes with laughter*]

BELLA

Don't start playing the hero. For starters I can't stand heroes. I wish all heroes
would kick it: they deserve to.

ISMAIL

It's funny your jewellery and your gun they don't go together.

BELLA

A prisoner shouldn't get personal.

That's how it is. That's how I've wanted to be.

My jewellery my mascara and my gun. My dad always used to say who'd want to make love with a bag of bones like me but I found someone who was really into bones. It didn't last long.

ISMAIL

Why?

BELLA

Any of your business?

ISMAIL

What do you want from me?

BELLA

I'm just chatting. Don't you like it?

ISMAIL

If we talk we talk and if we talk you put down your gun.

BELLA

That'll be the day when a guy pulls one over on me!

ISMAIL

I'm not trying to pull one over on you.

BELLA

Heard that one before.

ISMAIL

I haven't got a gun. You've got no reason to be suspicious.

BELLA

Being suspicious runs in my blood. They found my cousin's head in a sack outside my house. My family and the family across the field never stop taking pot-shots at each other. My grandfather my father my uncles it's been going on since long before I was born so there you are. What about you?

ISMAIL

I just happen to be here.

BELLA

The bullshit you come out with. Round here people "just happen" to wander round with grenades in their pockets.

ISMAIL

I haven't got any grenades in my pockets.

BELLA

How do I know that?

If you'd had a gun I'd have shot you down straight away. You'd have paid for what happened to the old woman.

ISMAIL

What's your name?

BELLA

What the fuck's it to you? My name's Bella. And yours?

ISMAIL

Ismail.

BELLA

That's a name and a half.

ISMAIL

I want to see you again.

BELLA

Nice one, kid. Thirty years from now when peace comes you and me we'll throw a big party. Only problem is - I'm warning you - we'll be old wrinklies by then.

ISMAIL

You're stupid.

BELLA

Word of advice, mate. Get the hell out of here. This is no place for you.

ISMAIL

Not for you either. Just a shitty rat-hole. Can we meet again?

BELLA

We'll see each other again. Maybe they've done away with frontiers in the land of the dead.

ISMAIL

Wait!

[She disappears. He runs off after her]

SEQUENCE 7

ZACK, the LITTLE OLD MAN, the LITTLE OLD WOMAN

[*Enter a dead man dressed in khakis GI-style, covered in blood and with dust from debris and plaster. This is ZACK*]

ZACK.

Maybe I shouldna said the word "cemetery"

cos that self-same second all Hell

broke loose the mother of all noises

the walls collapsed on top of us

and we was dead finito.

That hotel

Privileged View Of The War

just the kinda low-rent shithouse

I been hauling my ass thru these 15 years 'n' more.

You change continents

you trade in the jungle-bunnies for the greaseballs

so where's the difference.

The same ventilators always broke

the same crapped-out palm-trees

the same kids sizeing us up like we was already deadmeat

the same syphilitic carpets the same stoolpigeons

wiring a report every time you fart every time you burp down the telephone.

Yeh and yesterday an automobile blew up in that bitch of a parking-lot

not to mention their idea of "toast" in their negroid hotel

Call that "toast"? I call it aluminium.

There was serious backsheesh to be made with this dude

we closed the deal me I said 10 French AMX tanks

that's four million bucks

3300 pieces of 75 mill ammo and 25 other AMXs

that's 8,750, 000 bucks.

Just five foot from there supersnoop numero uno

dude goes by the name of The Lizard on account his tongue it's so pointy

he's leaning so far forward in his chair to listen

any second now I'm expecting him go fall flat on his face.

All these little crab-lice sucking our life-blood

in this shitty little cocksucker of a scabby scumbag war.
Right. So I gone put on the local pajamas I'm still spotted on account my red
hair right?
The guy tells me okay for the shekels
and that there'll be other orders if the er ... Political Risk-Factor Is Minimised.
You mean says I they'd be dumb enough
to declare peace?
Hell given the interests at stake that just ain't thinkable
The I-talians are re-servicing their tank-engines
The Norwegians are selling off their stocks of dynamite
The Krauts their so-called Agricultural Chemicals
The Switzers their Pilatus airplanes
The Chinks their missiles the Frenchies their AMX tanks
and you notice I ain't saying nothing about the Ruskies and the Yanks even ...
so when it comes to running a clock on markets like that one
hey pal that's ten billion dollars a year we're talking
hey big guy like you wanna kill the turkey that shits the golden eggs?
The politicos sure they mouth off like that bout cease-fires
just so's they can look cute on the TV
a pack of assholes of dickheads of fuckwits
cocksuckers ready to bend over for just one extra vote
but when it's down to stopping the war-market?
No way José.
Me I ain't scared of tomorrow domani manana
my god! my god!
Guys War is the one Field Of Endeavour that's still a growth-industry!
So this dude this kind of A-rab
just been bending my ear telling me I don't know the difference
between a detonator and a pressure-cooker.
Says you says I
me thinking another mother-fuckin' grease-ball
I say You gave me men don't understand diddly-shit.
Illiterate apes. I mean Illiterate A-rabs.
What you expect me to do?

Apes who don't understand electricity or plumbing
or mechanics let alone electronic arms.
I say These bozos o'yours they just got down off their camels.
He says You an expert in explosives or peanuts?
I say The real experts in explosives are guys
risk getting their ass blown away on the job.
He says You're supposed be ready blow away anything and everything you're
asked and you're supposed be ready blow up your own mother
be able make a bomb with just strawberry jam.
I say Hey let's not exaggerate Strawberries no ...
He says You's supposed be able stick a bomb under a postage-stamp.
Well? Is it yes... or No Go Fuck Yourself?
Me I'm wanting real bad say to this A-rab asshole Well that's too bad cos it's Just
No Go Fuck Yourself.
But Stay cool I'm telling myself this jerk has a djellabah shit-thick with
backsheesh
I say I can make 40 000 litres of explosives
with just the latest edition of the Koran!
At the word Koran this grease-ball comes on like he's spooked.
He says Make a list we'll get you what you want.
Even if we gotta send for a special plane from the US or the North Pole.
I say There's one more thing.
I was wasting my time explaining to your baboons
they handle explosives like they was crates of bananas.
When you take short-cuts with bombs
soon you got yourself a short-cut to the cemetery.
Maybe I shouldna said the word "cemetery"
cos that self-same second all Hell
broke loose the mother of all noises
the walls collapsed on top of us
and we was dead finito
a whole avalanche of rocks of dust
filling up our windpipes right down to our assholes.
The A-rab with the attaché-case smelling like a pansy
me and the crowd of grease-balls who've just got down off their camels

we was all blown up windpipes full of dust

scumbag Allah and his dickhead Paradise no one gonna convince me this round

here's any different from the shit I left down below.

Christ talk about dumb kicking it the day before

you 'bout to sign a contract gonna gild your balls in liquid gold.

One look round here you'd figure you was still in that shitty decor of their shitty

little sleazeball wars Pissed off

now I'm dead I wanna change of scenery

Hell I want some pussy bring on the belly-dancers a few angels maybe and music

and I want regular scenery with some real grass for Chrissake ...

[*He falls. The LITTLE OLD MAN and LITTLE OLD WOMAN return*]

LITTLE OLD MAN.

Ah. There you are. And later than scheduled. An inauspicious beginning to your
career in the Great Beyond, young man. Though it be written "No man shall
know the day nor the hour" that is no reason to be late.

LITTLE OLD WOMAN.

Leave him be. You can see he can't hear.

LITTLE OLD MAN.

That's normal. It's the shock. Yet another one not used to dying.

ZACK.

What's that? What's happening?

LITTLE OLD WOMAN.

Curtains. Finita la commedia.

ZACK.

What?

LITTLE OLD MAN.

You've just kicked the bucket.

LITTLE OLD WOMAN.

Popped your clogs. Shut up shop. Turned up your toes.

LITTLE OLD MAN.

Dropped off the twig. Cashed in your chips.

LITTLE OLD WOMAN.

Gone out feet first.

[*They choke with laughter*]

ZACK.

Where am I?

LITTLE OLD WOMAN.

Six feet under.

LITTLE OLD MAN.

Being fitted for a wooden overcoat.

Look how this one just can't let go.

LITTLE OLD WOMAN.

Old habits die hard.

ZACK.

So where are we?

LITTLE OLD WOMAN.

Where no one will try and sneak in ahead of you.

LITTLE OLD MAN.

Or let's just say you're in where you're out of it ...

[*They laugh*]

ZACK.

You two give me the creeps.

LITTLE OLD WOMAN.

Well, the fear of death never made death die ...

LITTLE OLD MAN.

Funny. They think they're learning how to live and they're learning how to die ...

[*They start to drag off the dead man*]

LITTLE OLD WOMAN.

When you were twenty and you made that trip to England who did you go with?

LITTLE OLD MAN.

On my own. I've told you two hundred thousand times. I went on my own.

LITTLE OLD WOMAN.

I might be very simple but there are some things ...

LITTLE OLD MAN.

Such as?

LITTLE OLD WOMAN.

Such as England. You've always lied to me about that. And yet it wouldn't be so very difficult just to say I was twenty years old and I made a trip to England with a girl ...

[*They drag off the dead man*]

SEQUENCE 8
KRIM, ISMAIL, BELLA, YONATHAN
The action takes place in two different parts of the stage.

IST SPACE
[*KRIM and ISMAIL seated on*
oil-drums in the middle of the ruins]

2ND SPACE
[*BELLA and YONATHAN grope in*
silence through the ruins]
BELLA
You pull out the cartridge-clip. Don't
look at me like that. You put me off.
YONATHAN
Like this?
BELLA
Yes. That's the breech-cover. You
release it like this. Pay attention to
what you're doing. You won't
remember anything.
YONATHAN
Right.
BELLA
One. The cartridge-clip. Two. The
breech-cover. Three. Bolt and breech
ring. Carry on. No not like that. Ah.
You're just a kid, aren't you. Four
kilos. A hundred shots a minute.
Cartridge-clip for thirty bullets at
seven hundred yards a second.
YONATHAN
Good.
BELLA
Careful. Don't press it. Watch out. It's
not a toy.

KRIM
Want a spliff?

ISMAIL
No.
KRIM
You should try.
You roll a spliff you get stoned
you dance to the radio
you get out of your head you can nick all
the cars you like you can blow away who
you want you're the king Rambo
Superman that's war
it's brilliant.
And then there's my Kalash when I hold it
against me she shakes me I'm
like some kinda nut when you've fired
once it's for life
it's the Real Thing there and then you
can't be without it ever again
when it spits you tremble from head to foot.
AKAKAKAKAKAKAK you really feel
the Devil he's not in man he's in the machine.
Come on, take this one.
I'm giving it to you. Your first Kalashnikov,
mate!
ISMAIL
No. I don't need it.
KRIM
The guy's crazy. Everyone
needs one, asshole.

BELLA
That little wall over there we'd be in a
good place.

KRIM
War there's nothing more
brilliant even girls can't
be more brilliant.

Anyway when it's all quiet it freaks me out.
When there's no gunfire I get
this terrible diarrhoea.
It's the same thing even with buddies.

BELLA
It gets clogged up with grease quickly
but it's a beauty.
Accurate up to 300 yards.

KRIM
Picture yourself with your helmet your
flak-jacket your mortar your
shades your Kalash

YONATHAN
But why should I fire?
BELLA
You don't seriously think we've
crossed the line for no good reason?
We've taken risks to get across this
fucking noman's land. Now we're
going to cop ourselves one or two.
YONATHAN
Why me?
BELLA
Come off it. You're from over there
and don't you forget it. So prove
yourself. Or else.
There's spies around. Gotta watch out.
Either you fire or I shoot you.
What did you think? That maybe it's all
a game?

ISMAIL
I'm too young for all that.
KRIM
If you weren't my buddy I'd

think you were shit-scared.
How old do you think they are over
there?

BELLA
Check the cartridge-clip. The safety-
catch. Stay cool. The first time it's
tough. You'll get used to it.

ISMAIL
What did your mother say the first time
she saw you in your khakis?
KRIM
You know what mothers are like. I was
twelve. I could handle my Kalash
better than I could my prick.
She slapped me, "Go get changed, this isn't
the movies." No, it's
war, I said. She slapped me again.
"you'll fight in the war when you're
a man and you're not a man at twelve."
So I'm getting into training while I wait I
said, and she slapped me again.
"Start like that and there's
no telling where you'll end up"
she said.

YONATHAN
And what if they're two of ours?
Two of our lot who've come over the
line like us?
BELLA
What if, what if, what if. You won't
hack it for long. I'm telling you, get
ready to fire. One thing you'll learn:
you shoot before you think -
otherwise you're already a dead man.

KRIM
If I have to wait till I can grow a beard
before I get to fight we'll all
be dead, I said.
She looks like she's going to slap me
again. So I shot off a round
through the window. That shut her up.
Now she jumps with joy
when I come back of an evening.

BELLA
Cool. Cool. Technique.
Technique. There. You've got one in
your sights. Just aim and stop thinking
about it.
YONATHAN
I can't.

KRIM
It's not complicated.
First – when you fight
it's you or the other guy, it's as
simple as that.
Second – if you see a
suspicious shadow you shoot first,
you shoot.
ISMAIL
And if it's a friend?
KRIM
Better shoot a friend
than get shot by an
enemy.
ISMAIL
It's crazy. I don't get it.

BELLA
Try not to shake.
What's wrong with you?

YONATHAN

There, opposite. One of those two is my mate. Ismail. It's Ismail. I can't shoot at Ismail. He's my oldest friend.

BELLA

Okay. So shoot at the other one.

Do you know the other one?

YONATHAN

I'm shaking too much. I can't.

BELLA

So breathe in like I said. Relax. Relax. Technique. A good killer's a good technician.

KRIM

I want to have a good time.

ISMAIL

Eat.

KRIM

Stuff ourselves you mean and make love in silk sheets.

ISMAIL

With real girls in real dresses.

KRIM

A rave up.

[*They start to move about like rock musicians*]

BELLA

Just remember one thing

We don't need spies or yellowbellies.

KRIM

My feet are getting tired.

My head's spinning.

I don't know how to dance any more.

BELLA

Now that's good. Shoot.

[*He fires*]

BELLA

You got him. You got him.

YONATHAN

What?

BELLA

You got him. You're good.

YONATHAN

It wasn't me. I didn't do anything.

It was an accident.

I fired and he fell.

It was an accident.

ISMAIL

Krim. Krim. Answer me, Krim.

Krim. Krim. Don't die, Krim.

Wait - you'll soon be better.

It's nothing. We'll go

to the hospital. We'll get you looked after.

A car. Quick. A car.

Krim I'm here. I'm here.

You're looking at me. Your eyes Krim.

A car. He's dead.

Krim wake up. I'm here.

Krim.

He's dead.

[*A passerby comes up to ISMAIL*]

PASSER BY

Was it you wanted a car?

ISMAIL

You were here. You were here all along.

You had a car.

You didn't budge.

What the fuck have you been up to all

this time? -

[*He takes the Kalashnikov and fires off a round into the stomach of the PASSER BY, who drops dead*]

ISMAIL

Krim. My first dead person.

A present for you. He's all yours.

Krim. Shit. Shit. Shit.

[*He throws down the Kalashnikov. He stays prostrate on KRIM's body. The silhouettes of the little old couple appear upstage*]

SEQUENCE 9

BELLA, ISMAIL, the LITTLE OLD MAN, the LITTLE OLD LADY

BELLA

You're still here.

ISMAIL

I knew I'd find you.

BELLA

Stop buzzing round me like a mosquito.

ISMAIL

My mate's dead.

BELLA

It happens.

ISMAIL

Yes.

BELLA

It happened to me too.

ISMAIL

Ah.

BELLA

Yes. He was called Yossif.

He was more than just a mate. Haven't talked about him for a long time.

ISMAIL

Tell me about him.

BELLA

Why should I.

ISMAIL

'Cos my mate's dead too.

BELLA.

So what. Okay. If you want.

When he went off to war I said to myself don't be so melodramatic

all the women in this country think the same bullshit as you're thinking at this

moment ... then their men come back.

One day I get a postcard. I'm happy to see his handwriting. But then silence and

more silence.

I couldn't imagine him killing anyone. What about you - have you killed anyone?

ISMAIL

The first time I killed it was for my mate.
The second was for my little brother, the third for my father, the fourth for my mother. After that I stopped counting.

BELLA

Right. What was I saying?

ISMAIL

Silence.

BELLA

I wrote every day no answer. Then one Friday two men in plain clothes at the door. I stuffed my hand in my mouth and bit into it. He'd died February 4th and already been buried two days. I didn't cry. They gave me some water and I looked at the glass shaking in my hand.

ISMAIL

And afterwards?

BELLA

It's afterwards it gets tricky. That same evening I asked a friend to take me out. I had to get out. We walked round town. It was curfew. I wanted to say "Take me in your arms. Touch me." I didn't dare. He wouldn't haveunderstood. I don't like you looking at me when I talk about it.

ISMAIL

It's almost dark. I can't see you. Carry on.

BELLA

I bumped into one of my girlfriends - we were kids together. It turned out she'd been a war-widow for six years. I wanted to scream. I swore I'd never get like her. I'm not some monument to the dead. I know some who've gone mad. So - then and there - snap out of it, no more moping. My dresses my make-up my jewelry. The pain down here that's nobody's business. Every night I dream I'm dead. It helps.

ISMAIL

Take me in your arms.

BELLA

You've never touched a woman, have you?

ISMAIL

No never.

BELLA

It's funny. I've always had very simple problems that got complicated the longer I didn't deal with them. Problems with love, of affection, all that stuff. I'd like a good dose of sex to make me forget it all.

ISMAIL

That's easy. Kiss me.

They kiss.

BELLA

Now go away.

ISMAIL

Why? I want to ...

BELLA

I know what you want. Piss off.

ISMAIL

I've never slept with a woman. I've fired off five thousand rockets but I've never slept with a woman. I've done it all -- but I've never done it with a woman.

BELLA

"When the winter is cold the porcupines try and warm each other up by hugging each other but each one's prickles dig into the flesh of the other one and scratch. So the porcupines separate and start feeling cold again."

That's how it is between a guy from your side and a girl from mine.

Piss off. I'll count up to three then I'll shoot.

ISMAIL

You wouldn't do that.

BELLA

One.

ISMAIL

Shoot what do I care?

BELLA

Two.

ISMAIL

Bitch.

BELLA

Three.

[*He runs off. She fires in the air. Then goes. The little old couple pass*]

LITTLE OLD MAN

Another young one?

LITTLE OLD WOMAN

What difference does it make?

You only had to read the orders.

35 years old, six children. No professional qualifications.

LITTLE OLD MAN

More orphans.

LITTLE OLD WOMAN

The mother's still alive.

LITTLE OLD MAN

One more widow.

LITTLE OLD WOMAN

Every silver lining...

LITTLE OLD MAN

This one's polite, at least.

Punctual when it comes to dying.

SEQUENCE 10

[*A DEAD MAN covered in mud from head to toe slowly emerges from the earth till he is standing upright. He has difficulty speaking. First he has to spit out the earth which fills his mouth then wipe the mud from his eyes, his nose, his ears*]

DEAD MAN COVERED IN MUD

Salam Aleikoum.

I died yesterday.I was still alive when they buried me.

I've lived in the desert I've kicked around from Hoggar to Tibesti.

With my father I witnessed sandstorms in the Ténéré.

One day I buried my son in a sack stamped "Wheatflour

Gift of the German Federal Republic".

I carried his dead body for days and days

I was looking for a city I thought

perhaps in the cities the hospitals perform miracles

but my son was dead and already shrivelled up in my arms.

I wrapped him in this German flour-sack

and I buried him amidst other unknown dead people

and I marked the grave with an old piece of a car a camshaft. There's no wood to

mark graves with in the desert.

Everything is parched. The earth is parched.

Women's breasts are empty and parched.

And everywhere these people wandering along trails

these epidemics.

And the desert they say that it's a living thing

that every day it eats up another three miles.

I wanted to leave this place where corpses are like milestones lining the trails.

I had to find money to feed my six kids.

I crossed a lot of frontiers at night

a little suitcase on my head.

Don't ask me how I ended up here.

I got taken on as a labourer.

I'm not a soldier I've got six children

and this war of theirs is nothing to do with me. Their war means nothing to me.

And it's none of my business.

Just when my contract was up and they were due to pay me for the six months
the police came to see me they said "You've got a choice. Either
we deport you and you go home without a penny
or you go to the front for just three short months
and then you get paid."
I couldn't go home unpaid
my wife would have chucked me out.
And so I went off to fight at this front of theirs
I didn't know how to hold a rifle.
I was taken on a truck-ride, no idea where we were going.
They said it didn't matter. You just shoot at what's in front of you
that's all there is to it.
There were fifty of us like that in my unit
there so we'd get paid for the work we'd done
repair-men electricians plumbers labourers.
They'd taken our passports away.
One day the other side took us prisoner.
They thought it was a great laugh.
They wouldn't believe us we told them
that we were there by chance
that we knew nothing about this war
that we were there just so we could collect the pay we were owed.
These guys from the other side this cracked them up they couldn't believe it
they beat us with clubs
and kicked us in the guts again and again
and stretched us out half K.O. side by side
face down in the ground.
During all this a bulldozer blockaded the village
with a heap of rocks so people wouldn't see
what they were going to do to us.
In the space of a few seconds it all flashed in front of me
the camels the date-palms the caravans
the eyes of the Tuaregs Hoggar Tibesti
my grandfather singlehanded taking on a squadron of French bayonets
and the desert cemetery

I won't even have a camshaft on my tomb.
The bulldozer charged down on top of us
it dumped sand and more sand and more sand
and I felt it was all over and finished
a guy was shouting squash them flat squash them flat
the dozer charged down on us those who were shouting were choked to death
mouths full of sand.
Those who ran away were cut down by the wheels of the bulldozer
those who stayed put motionless with fear
were crushed and hurled in the air and thrown back
into the earth like a root you're planting
and serves us right for being taught to defend other people's land
that land it came right down on top of us.

[*Exhausted, he falls motionless to the ground*]

LITTLE OLD MAN

He's too heavy to lift.

Please try. Get up.

DEAD MAN

Where am I?

LITTLE OLD MAN

It's very tiresome. They all come out with the same thing.

LITTLE OLD WOMAN.

What do you expect. Every job has its routine.

THE DEAD MAN

Where am I?

LITTLE OLD WOMAN.

Oh dear me, here we go again. Six feet under, a wooden overcoat ...

LITTLE OLD MAN

It's funny. They think they're learning to live but ...

LITTLE OLD WOMAN.

Yes, yes, you said that before too.

[*They leave dragging the dead man behind them as best they can*]

SEQUENCE 11

ISMAIL, BELLA

BELLA

Curl up here in my smell. I feel good.

ISMAIL

Your left breast fits my right hand perfectly.

BELLA

I'm pregnant Ismail.

ISMAIL

You think this is a good time?

BELLA

You don't choose the time.

I went to the cemetery where all my family is

and I said, you dead out there, listen to me and give me a son.

They listened to me.

ISMAIL

I killed today.

BELLA

Right. It's their war, let them sort it out. The cats eat the rats. I don't feel like a

cat or a rat.

ISMAIL

Shut up you fool. You're asking for trouble.

Get rid of it.

You don't have a baby with bombs dropping all around you. Your breasts are

too small.

You won't get any milk.

BELLA

No.

Later it'll say

what have you done with the perfume, the music, the lilacs.

Once upon a time everywhere round here smelled of lilacs.

Today not so much as a tree.

And what kind of answer will I give it?

ISMAIL

You won't give it any answer because you're going to get rid of it.

BELLA

You're a man. You don't understand a thing. Not even a man, a snotty kid. To find something that would get me out of my head for just one moment all I had was my belly. You, you wouldn't mind if the war lasted for ever. Well - isn't that right?

ISMAIL

I wouldn't mind if you shut up.

BELLA

Keep away from me.

ISMAIL

I don't want to.

BELLA

You think that's a good enough reason.

Don't look at me like that. I don't like being looked at.

ISMAIL

Come here where it's dark.

No one will see you.

[*They go out*]

SEQUENCE 12

MOTHER HEN, the DEAD MAN covered in seaweed and kerosene, the LITTLE OLD MAN, the LITTLE OLD WOMAN.

MOTHER HEN

I knew how to sow and dig - knew how to work the soil - and also - my old man was a shoemaker - how to strip the leather from its fur scrape it clean prepare for the tanning when you flay it.

When the old man came over impotent after our fourteenth I was really disappointed.

We'd been doing really well up to then:

two boys one girl two boys one girl

like knit two purl one knit two purl one.

That gave us exactly ten boys and four girls.

I had milk all the time.

In the village they called me Mama Fourteen-Tits

and I was proud of it.

I wanted my boys to become monks

To have all the good things in life the oven the farms the wine-press the rents the tithes and the orchards and pot-bellies and paunches and preserved fruit in their monasteries. All except two who I'd have kept to be married off. And the girls I'd have married off too.

They buried my husband in God's little square.

That's the pauper's spot near the church.

And all it needed was that disaster that mania for Jerusalem

Farewell monasteries my sons farewell husbands for my daughters.

It's mad to have big ideas for your kids.

Walking walking walking.

I was afraid of reaching the sea.

They said it would separate down the middle like it did in the past

for Moses.

And we'd walk on completely dry between two walls of hanging water.

Well you'll never believe this the sea didn't separate down the middle!

We had to go round the edge of that endless sea.

God is testing us said Etienne it's proof He loves us.

If that was his way of loving us, well, he really did love us.

I've been walking for eight hundred years now.

It's nothing - a straw in the wind. But what if it was the weight of this straw which broke the camel's back when he was tired?

I'm at the end of my tether but not the end of my journey.

I haven't got any shoes left I haven't even got any feet left.

[*Enter a DEAD MAN covered in seaweed and kerosene. His clothes are soaked. His face is blue*]

DEAD MAN

Our boat was torpedoed by an Exocet.

MOTHER HEN

All that rubbish here we go again.

DEAD MAN

The tanker's ripped to pieces in no time.

The hull vibrates and rings out like a bell.

The speakers scream. Everything on board capsizes.

Fire breaks out in the engine-room

you throw yourself on the ground

the extinguishers don't work.

A sickening smoke spreads everywhere. My hands began to tremble.

We drift stuck on that hulk for months.

I get giddy spells and pains right down in my bones.

Water's rationed - two bucketfuls a day for twenty men -

I'm so thirsty my tongue's all cracked

we're suffocating thanks to the petrol-fumes

we throw up several times a night we're sick as dogs

it's 46 degrees on board during the day and almost

as much at night.

MOTHER HEN

So what do you want. What's your name for a start?

DEAD MAN

My name's irrelevant I'm trash and rubbish.

Where I come from we're called the untouchables.

I've always been in rags and tatters slept in shit-heaps

with beggars, vomit and rotting flesh.

Even our shadows dirty what they touch.

Our sin is to have been born untouchable.

We're only allowed the skins of dead animals

to cut them up to beat them to spread quicklime on them by hand

to wring them out to sew them to dry them to make shoes out of them.

My body would burn up from mixing the quicklime.

One night in the monsoon season my mother went mad

she slapped herself violently several times

she put cowdung in her hair

she started laughing and laughing

she didn't stop laughing till she died.

I set off on foot my whole life rotting away.

In secret I embarked on a ship leaving for the Gulf.

What Gulf. People always said The Gulf.

It was a kid who sunk us. A kamikaze

on a boat made of plastic so the radar wouldn't pick him up.

The kid the boat and the tanker all went up at the same moment.

[*The DEAD MAN drops dead. The LITTLE OLD MAN enters*]

LITTLE OLD MAN

A real chatterbox, that one.

LITTLE OLD WOMAN *entering*

No more of a chatterbox than the others.

LITTLE OLD MAN.

He's the only one I've listened to.

MOTHER HEN

Exocet ... Kamikaze ... I don't understand a thing.

LITTLE OLD WOMAN

Where did you get to? We've got work to do.

LITTLE OLD MAN

But you're the one who's late.

I tell you sometimes I want to chuck it all in.

All these dead people. The same old story.

LITTLE OLD WOMAN

Don't forget we're lucky to have a job at all.

Most of them have to put up with eternal boredom ...

[*They go off dragging the dead man behind them*]

SEQUENCE 13

BELLA, ISMAIL, the LITTLE OLD WOMAN, the LITTLE OLD MAN

[BELLA is nine months pregnant]

ISMAIL

The real buzz is when you shoot down a car just like in the movies.

The car races on you feel the guys inside it going spare

in their coffin on wheels it's brilliant

here in the middle of this desert with the heat

making everything shimmy. The car's got one chance in ten of making it.

You've got several rifles all aiming at it. The driver throws the wheel to the right

then the left. The car is like it's arseholed it's getting nearer. I've got the driver in

my sights. I focus. Fire! It skids. It ends up against a concrete block. It explodes in

a squirt of flames. Four ghosts on fire run in different directions. They collapse.

It's over.

BELLA

You've become a killer. It's disgusting.

ISMAIL

Call it what you like.

BELLA

Your head's like your heart is - nobody home.

ISMAIL

Not quite. War's taught me things.

BELLA

What for example?

ISMAIL

How to defend myself. A woman hanging up her laundry the other side of the

line. I shoot. Everything that moves is the enemy.

[BELLA spits into the ground]

BELLA

I'm not spitting in your face

because you're might be the father of what I've got in my belly.

ISMAIL

Might be?

BELLA

What do you think?

Since Yossif died I've needed lots of men to forget.

ISMAIL

You're a whore.

BELLA

Call it what you like.

ISMAIL

Piss off.

BELLA

What the fuck's it to you who I sleep with. You don't love me.

ISMAIL

Yes I do. You're the only woman I've ever touched.

BELLA

So listen for once: any man who's in love with me is a fool because he loves a cow and a slut.

ISMAIL

Piss off. Whore. Piss off. Before I shoot.

BELLA

Shoot. It'll prove you've got balls.

ISMAIL

I can't.

BELLA

So the killer chickens out.

ISMAIL

I want to make love.

BELLA

Never again, you hear? Too much blood – the blood of my people – on your skin.

ISMAIL

You weren't always so disgusted.

BELLA

You weren't always an assassin.

ISMAIL

It's the war it's not me ...

BELLA

You'd say the same about a guy on the other side who'd killed your mate for instance?

ISMAIL

What are you getting at?

BELLA

You remember the day Krim was shot.

ISMAIL

I'm not gaga. I've got a memory.

BELLA

He was shot by M16 bullets in this part of town.

ISMAIL

What are you getting at?

BELLA

And just after that you shot a guy who'd been a bit slow lending you his car.

ISMAIL

How do you know that?

BELLA

I was there. I saw it all.

ISMAIL

And may we ask what the fuck you were doing there?

BELLA

Right. Not only did I see it all. I was with a guy. He had to prove himself. He came from your part of town. It was me made him kill Krim.

ISMAIL

No.

BELLA

Oh yes. And this guy's your pal Yonathan.

[ISMAIL shoots her. She falls. She's covered with blood. The dead BELLA stands up again]

BELLA

I'm trying to knit the bits of my face together again.

I give it a good rub. It looks like it's all in one piece.

In fact there's a crack in it. It's not there any more. It's not my face any more I've lost it. I'm dead.

No more petrol no more electricity no more post no more planes no more
trains. Life was going back five centuries but for nine months
I was going forward against the tide. I measured time by the size of my belly
poor madwoman that I was. Poor lunatic.
You were in my belly you were ready your head all lined up where it was
supposed to be
and in my head
it was Summer.
I'd always been less of a woman than other women
and here I was finally getting round finally feeling
the most womenly of women. Poor fool.
I made you. You're here.
Everyone take cover! And my belly the best cover of all.
And every evening those naked men turned on by the war pressed up against me.
And you were ready and finished at last.
My cunt hurts. My cunt was about to open.
I already felt it, it was time for us to part.
There's a complete blank in my head.
An iron curtain is cutting my head in two.
My brain feels like the propellor of a plane chopping through fog.
I felt you and me we'd separate
I felt my milk rising
the waters in my belly got ready to break
I wanted you to come out
and to leave a little trace inside me
like a knife on the bark of a tree.
You're not moving any more. It's not moving any more.
It's not too late.
Please: try.
He was still living a few minutes after I died.
It's not too late.
A child can be born from a dead woman.
Cut me in two.

Open my belly up, down the middle.

So it can get out.

I beg you.

Don't let it rot inside my corpse.

[*Exhausted she falls motionless*]

ISMAIL

Bella!

LITTLE OLD MAN.

What a waste. If he'd waited just one more hour that child would be born.

LITTLE OLD WOMAN

Well he was right not to wait. That child will be better off with us than with them.

LITTLE OLD MAN.

All the same. To have died without seeing Venice ...

LITTLE OLD WOMAN

You and your bar-room philosophy.

I would have so loved to go travelling. If you hadn't been allergic

to suitcases we would have gone everywhere.

LITTLE OLD MAN.

You're the one who says that. You who's afraid of snakes, spiders, mice, cats, rats, dentists, doctors, blood ...

LITTLE OLD WOMAN

Seen the cave-dwellers in undiscovered parts of Africa. The pygmies.

LITTLE OLD MAN.

There aren't any left.

LITTLE OLD WOMAN

Headed west whole days on camel-back. Slept on rush-matting in bamboo huts. Walked in the mud, the swamps, through clouds of insects and the roar of lions, and in an unbearable stench of slime ruined our umbrellas in the violence of tropical rain-storms ...

LITTLE OLD MAN.

You who can't stand the damp or the smell of insect-repellant ...

LITTLE OLD WOMAN

I'd have liked to go into outer space. See all those suns close up, those planets, those stars, those galaxies ...Do you think one day we'll build cathedrals on the moon.

LITTLE OLD MAN.

You're interested in the moon and you're not interested in me.

LITTLE OLD WOMAN

But there's no comparison.

LITTLE OLD MAN.

Give me your hand.

LITTLE OLD WOMAN

You're big enough now to walk all by yourself.

LITTLE OLD MAN.

Don't let go of me. You're going too fast. Everything's going too fast. Don't leave me. The sky's an unbearable blue. The noise is unbearable ...
The horizon ...

LITTLE OLD WOMAN

It's nothing. A little guerrilla fire.

LITTLE OLD MAN.

You're going too fast.

LITTLE OLD WOMAN

Hurry up. You always dawdling like that it wears me out in the end.
[*She leaves*]

THE LITTLE OLD MAN.

Where are you?

You shouldn't have let go of my hand.

Where are you going in such a rush? Why are you running? We've got all the time in the world ...

I shouldn't have let you leave. You'll be frightened all on your own.

I've forgotten my name.

It'll come back. I haven't lost my memory. Proof: I

remember when we used to make love you'd be scratching yourself all the time.

What's the point of being the only one left to remember.

It's really night now.

I also remember our first evening and our second evening and all the evenings which followed ... Where are you?

It's your bad luck if I forget you ...

You shouldn't have let go of my hand.

I'll start a new life. Yes that's it. Each morning it's a new world. I'll go to the brothel. Yes that's it to the brothel. I'll fornicate.

Is that the sun or more of those fires.

The rubbish-collectors will come by soon.

Without you here it's as stupid as dying.

I'll find you again. I've plenty of time.

Since we died there have already been new leaves on the trees and litters of kittens which have had kittens in their turn and houses built and babies and plenty of coffins.

I'll find you.

I stumbled and you didn't wait for me.

There are two ways to live: the ordinary and the extraordinary.

Without you it'll just be the ordinary but that won't last.

I don't know my name any more but I remember how you smell ...

[*The LITTLE OLD MAN leaves. Meanwhile BELLA's corpse has mysteriously disappeared. Quick blackout*]

SEQUENCE 14

ISMAIL, YONATHAN, the LITTLE OLD MAN and LITTLE OLD WOMAN

[*YONATHAN enters. He is blind. ISMAIL has a leg wrapped in dirty rags. He is limping*]

ISMAIL

Yonathan!

YONATHAN.

Ismail. Is that you? It's your voice. Ismail.

ISMAIL

No. Over here. Careful. The whole area's thick with landmines.

What are you doing. Not over there.

Can't you see the mines?

YONATHAN.

I'm blind.

ISMAIL

What did you say?

YONATHAN.

It dazzled me. A thousand suns.

A phosporescent bomb.

My eyelids melted. They stuck together. I'm blind.

ISMAIL

Careful. Keep still. There. Next to you. A mine.

YONATHAN.

Come and get me.

ISMAIL

Don't move an inch. Stop. You'll get yourself blown up.

You're just a few inches from a mine.

To your left.

YONATHAN.

Come and get me.

ISMAIL

Easy for you to say. I can't move.

I'm practically dead. I've lost a leg.

And half my blood.

And then it swelled up, it turned black. I wrapped it in rags. It was going pus-sy.

No, you fool. Yonathan! Not there! To your left! To your left I said!

YONATHAN.

My left or your left?

We must be opposite each other. So my left is your right.

ISMAIL

It's your right then. No. Don't move any more. Stop.

Are you deaf or what.

YONATHAN.

My right or your right. I don't understand.

ISMAIL

Your right.

YONATHAN.

Like this? Here? Can I get to you this way?

ISMAIL

Yes. But don't move a hair on either side.

YONATHAN.

I'm scared of falling over.

Still all right? There are no mines here, are there?

ISMAIL

No. Go straight ahead.

[*They meet. They hug*]

ISMAIL

Yonathan.

YONATHAN.

Ismail.

ISMAIL

I thought we were fucked. That we'd never see each other again.

YONATHAN.

You're all thin.

ISMAIL

No more than you.

YONATHAN.

But you look heavy.

ISMAIL

No. Don't eat for a week – that's how light I am.

YONATHAN.

    Heavier than a crate of shells.

    if you don't eat, that means whole months without having a shit.

ISMAIL

    The noise gives me diarrhoea. But the smoke makes me constipated.

    The way it must work, the shit goes back into my blood and feeds me a second

    time round otherwise I'd have died of hunger by now.

    What happened to your eyes?

YONATHAN.

    I crossed over the line twice.

    The first time we lost but I kept my sight.

    The second time we won but I lost my eyes.

ISMAIL

    You've changed.

YONATHAN.

    You too.

    We're like two old men. I've seen it all except love.

ISMAIL

    Lucky you. Love's the pits.

YONATHAN.

    What do you mean? Explain.

ISMAIL

    No. Let's talk about something else. Your mother.

YONATHAN.

    Dead. And yours?

ISMAIL

    Same. Let's talk about something else.

YONATHAN.

    Like what?

ISMAIL

    Like us.

YONATHAN.

    There's nothing to talk about. Apart from the war.

ISMAIL

    Same for me.

YONATHAN.

What happened, Ismail?

ISMAIL

Nothing. Nothing happened.

[*They throw themselves into each other's arms. ISMAIL abruptly moves away*]

ISMAIL

We mustn't. We're enemies.

YONATHAN.

No.

ISMAIL

You went over to the other side.

YONATHAN.

Yes. But.

ISMAIL

You're an enemy.

YONATHAN.

If you like.

ISMAIL

An enemy.

YONATHAN.

Not *your* enemy.

ISMAIL

An enemy of my people is my enemy.

YONATHAN.

Ismail.

ISMAIL

That's how it is. You made your choice.

YONATHAN.

I'm not your enemy.

ISMAIL

You're on the other side.

YONATHAN.

If you like.

ISMAIL

Go away.

YONATHAN.

You want me to walk across that set of landmines again?

ISMAIL

You have to. The enemy, they're where you come from.

And the enemy, they're the other side of those mines.

YONATHAN.

Be my guide.

[*ISMAIL picks up his Kalashnikov and aims at YONATHAN. A pause as if he's hesitating*]

ISMAIL

There you are. That's it. Straight ahead.

[*He fires. Yonathan collapses. YONATHAN - now dead - stands up and speaks*]

YONATHAN.

They came to get me. They left me no choice.

Either you're with us or we take your gun away.

Taking my gun away would be like killing me. I said Okay.

I wanted to keep my distance stay out of it a bit.

The streets were blocked by jeeps with field-guns on them.

That part of town was sealed off we could cover the houses from the motorway.

Heavy artillery on every hilltop.

They were like rats in a trap.

The people down below were waiting for the massacre.

Three whole days they waited like that for the massacre to begin.

We pounded them with whole tons of bombs.

Our orders: liquidate. Liquidate all of them.

We killed in all sorts of ways.

M16s Kalashnikovs grenades machine-guns MPKs

rocket-launchers anti-tank grenades chucked into the people

52 mortars Soviet rifles side-arms

even those stones you swing above your head at the end of a piece of string. We

killed with our bare hands.

You snap a man's neck you break backbones you

strangle with rope made of nylon you stab a knife in chests

you paralyse with a needle in the neck

with your knife you aim at arteries
and veins and under the collar-bone and of course at the heart.
It takes between ten seconds and three minutes for death to happen.
There are some places to aim at which are really worth it the eyes the genitals.
The eyes thay're a doddle. The genitals they're tougher.
The guy it's like he feels he's fucking coming when you stick your knife in his prick.
Not a pretty sight.
The most difficult thing to do is to cut the throat of a man who's still alive.
You mustn't waste a single slash of the knife and it's best to do it from behind.
Playing the hero is pointless.
We've booby-trapped cars doors cigarette-packets
jerrycans stuffed with TNT we've fired fired fired
even on kids because they grow up and one day
they'll shoot you in the back.
Helicopters dropped clusters of missiles
the camp burned the vines burned across miles of hills
stone-walls exploded.
It only takes 48 hours and then you're finished with the bombs the explosions
the human pulp.
Hang on in there hang on in there just a bit further till the end
whole bunches of kids would throw themselves under the tanks
they were crushed to death whole groups of them
others set on fire with flame-throwers
human torches still running for another hundred yards.
All for one more second of life.
Blood filling your hands clothes eyes walls.
Slaughter slaughter slaughter.
KERPOW! The other guy falls you step over him you don't see anything any more you move forward a corpse falls on top of you explodes into bits and pieces all cut to shreds and splashing you in a shower of blood.
At every step children in little bits babies their heads bust open
disembowelled women holding on to their children
you're like an animal it's them or you

fire - bang!- at anything that moves a kid a cat a pal.

Bang bang bang save your skin bang bang bang bang.

[*He falls and does not move. The LITTLE OLD MAN and LITTLE OLD WOMAN are face to face*]

LITTLE OLD MAN.

It's you. I knew it.

I never believed you'd really left. Never.

You're beautiful. You're more beautiful than the five proofs of the existence of God. You are the proof of the existence of God.

LITTLE OLD WOMAN

We're up to our ankles in mud and blood and you've got time to pay compliments ...

LITTLE OLD MAN.

I'm Thirst and you are Water ...

LITTLE OLD WOMAN

Listen. There's revolution in the air and almost certainly a religious war. I no longer know who abdicated there's a junta a coup d'état in short time's ripe for a revolution perhaps even a proletarian one to sum up it all looks ultra-serious. Let's say a civil war turning into a world war or something more complicated but that's all I know and you've gone and put on your tattered trousers ...

LITTLE OLD MAN.

When things go badly they talk of Fate and when it's going well they talk of Politics.

Actually, nothing's certain except love.

LITTLE OLD WOMAN

What's the point of talking if you're only going to talk nonsense ...

LITTLE OLD MAN.

I'm getting tired.

LITTLE OLD WOMAN

We've been a bit overworked recently.

LITTLE OLD MAN.

I think I've lost weight. The day we got marrried we didn't weigh a hundred kilos the two of us put together ... Do you remember?

SEQUENCE 15

YONATHAN, ISMAIL, the LITTLE OLD MAN and LITTLE OLD WOMAN,
MOTHER HEN, ZACK, the DEAD MAN covered in seaweed, BELLA.
[*MOTHER HEN enters. She sees the ruins for the first time*]

MOTHER HEN

Don't tell me this is Jerusalem.

It can't be Jerusalem.

Etienne used to say Jerusalem was a beauty-spot on the face of the world.

ISMAIL

I'm in pain.

MOTHER HEN

You're in pain?

So am I. You get used to it.

Do you want me to sing you something?

Just for you. I never sing. But just for you? Okay.

As you wish.

I know which herbs can heal but round here ...

Not a single plant in all the rubble and ruins.

Show me. That looks nasty.

ISMAIL

My leg.

MOTHER HEN

Dear me, yes ... your leg.

There's not much left of it. Your leg stayed behind to fight the war.

[*She moves towards ISMAIL. He picks up his Kalshnikov and aims at MOTHER HEN*]

ISMAIL

Stay right there.

MOTHER HEN

What kind of country is this where the children are old.

Drop that gun. Don't be a fool.

Even an animal's got more sense than you.

LITTLE OLD MAN

[*To the LITTLE OLD WOMAN*]

Now he's going to die.

LITTLE OLD WOMAN
That's life.
LITTLE OLD MAN
Sometimes you let yourself be touched by it all. You'd like – I don't know – to
freeze, to postpone, to leave things hanging for one moment longer.
LITTLE OLD WOMAN
One moment more or less ...
LITTLE OLD MAN
It can make all the difference.
For me to have died one minute before meeting you would have meant a life
empty of meaning. Whereas one minute later ... Just one single minute ...
ISMAIL
Hell, what do I care.
[He drops his Kalashnikov]
I'm in pain.
I stink. My whole body's rotten meat.
I haven't washed for months.
And you're just part of my fever.
You don't exist.
[He hits himself several times]
I can still see you.
MOTHER HEN
Drink.
[ZACK enters]
ZACK.
Talk about dumb kicking it like that the day before
a contract gonna gild your balls in liquid gold.
Pissed off. Now I'm dead.
I wanna change of scenery.
Hell I want some pussy bring on the belly-dancers a few angels maybe and music
I want regular scenery with some real grass
I don't wanna spend my death here.
MOTHER HEN
[To ISMAIL]
How did you do that?

ISMAIL

A helicopter. It was hovering fifteen yards above the ground. The noise of the propellors, the sand thrown up by the bombs, the machine-gun and the grenades. I got scared.

ZACK

At least after I've got the right to some proper scenery.

I'm gonna complain to God.

And for a kick-off just where is he?

Hey! God! Where you gone? Where you gone God?

Hey! God! I'm letting ya know I'm dead!

ISMAIL

I was there right under the big monster with my little rifle

like a kid playing at killing an elephant

with a water-pistol.

[*The DEAD MAN covered in seaweed enters*]

DEAD MAN COVERED IN SEAWEED

I died in this Gulf full of oil-tankers and helicopters boats Exocets and Kamikazes Americans diplomats.

I died from exhaustion.

I was thrown into the water at 15:40. My corpse drifts slowly in the oily waters of the Gulf.

[*He falls exhausted, motionless*]

LITTLE OLD MAN

Why do they all want to come out of that grave of theirs?

They don't even have the strength to stand upright.

MOTHER HEN

[*To ISMAIL*]

I'm going to cauterize your wound. There's no alternative.

Grit your teeth.

ZACK

For Chrissake. Come and pass judgement on me.

Come on. Now's the time. I've been baptised. I paid the priest to do it.

God I'm calling out to you. This is a dead man calling out to you.

MOTHER HEN

Not so much noise.

There are people round here who are wounded.

ZACK

So what. Me I'm dead.

[*YONATHAN enters*]

ISMAIL

Yonathan!

YONATHAN

I found a guy under a bed.

I got him by the hair. He was yelling.

I stuck a knife in his back.

My hand went in and in and in.

ISMAIL

Yonathan!

He doesn't recognise me.

MOTHER HEN

He's blind. He looks all feverish.

Hey you, stop moving around so much.

ZACK

It's my right.

I want the angels, judgement, the flaming sword,

everything as promised, the whole shebang.

LITTLE OLD MAN

When I talk about love either you don't hear me

or you tell me I'm repeatin myself.

It's the deaf talking to the dumb.

LITTLE OLD WOMAN

To understand each other without speaking a single word – that's worth waiting

a whole lifetime for.

Now you should be getting on with those people there.

LITTLE OLD MAN

They've escaped. They're dead people on the run.

LITTLE OLD WOMAN

That's to be expected.

The cemetery was churned up by the bombs.

ISMAIL

Yonathan. Listen to me.

He's got it in for me 'cos I killed him.

You saw things without understanding them.

The column of kids all draped in white

the AMX tanks their engines just ticking over.

MOTHER HEN

Don't move so much.

ISMAIL

The kids tied a rope between their feet

so they couldn't run away at the last minute.

They took each other's hands and set off towards the minefield ...

LITTLE OLD MAN

This is getting out of hand.

All the dead are coming back. Flooding back.

[*ZACK shoots*]

LITTLE OLD MAN

Cease fire!

Cease fire!

Stop shooting!

In this place we have to make peace.

ZACK

I'll stop when those opposite stop.

LITTLE OLD MAN

You don't understand you're dead.

ZACK

So? Dead or not dead I've always kept my ass well covered.

YONATHAN

Survive. Advance. Kill. Kill. Kill.

ZACK

Shit, haven't I always worn a crucifix round my neck?

Give us a sign for fuck's sake. You don't exist. Admit it. You don't exist for fuck's sake.

God God God God.

[*He falls motionless*]

ISMAIL

The kids kept straight on
you could see the mines half buried
the first wave of them was blown up
arms legs childrens' heads
flying in all directions
a whole horizon of legs of arms of children's heads.

MOTHER HEN

Shut up. It's just your fever.

ISMAIL

No. I saw it.

MOTHER HEN

Shut up anyway.

YONATHAN

kill kill kill survive escape chop lop down kill kill kill ...

[*He falls motionless*]

MOTHER HEN

God spares me nothing.

LITTLE OLD MAN

They're mad. The dead have gone mad.

LITTLE OLD WOMAN

How could they when they're dead.

ISMAIL

The first wave of them was blown up you'd hear a few very soft groans kids who weren't completely dead
even in pieces you can live on a bit.
That was like a signal we revved the tank engines
we moved on over the ground filled with pieces of kids
the little bodies squirted in the mud the metal
others sunk in the soft soil.
Some lay dying their mouths full of earth.

The kids had set the mines off.

Now the tanks could get across.

[*Enter BELLA*]

ISMAIL

Bella!

BELLA

If you let yourself be eaten up by grief it rots your insides and kills you.

Every night those men

who wouldn't even take off their khakis ...

Some of them when they came into me they were cold

like instruments.

ISMAIL

Bella!

She can't see me.

LITTLE OLD MAN

She's dead.

MOTHER HEN

What a hellish journey.

The closer you get to the promised land the less it looks like one.

LITTLE OLD MAN

All the dead have been smitten with insomnia ...

LITTLE OLD WOMAN

Let's not get upset.

Life, death, all these dramas ... we mustn't make a tragedy out of them.

LITTLE OLD MAN

Let's sleep. Let's try to sleep.

LITTLE OLD WOMAN

Let's wake up again in two hundred years' time.

LITTLE OLD MAN

What for?

LITTLE OLD WOMAN

Just to see ...

[*Leaning against each other they fall asleep*]

BELLA

This whole horizon of blazing fires. These false Messiahs, these real missiles.

We all die of asphyxiation in this airless country.

I'd made this child like an old man plants a tree,

poor fool that I was ...

[*She falls motionless*]

ISMAIL

Bella wake up. Speak to me. Bella!

MOTHER HEN

Shut up.

[*An enormous explosion lights up the entire sky. MOTHER HEN is in the middle of the plateau littered with the dead. ZACK, YONATHAN, The DEAD MAN covered in seaweed, the LITTLE OLD MAN, the LITTLE OLD WOMAN, BELLA*]

MOTHER HEN

That smell of dead bodies and burning ...

How's your leg. The stench turns my stomach inside out.

ISMAIL

I'm in pain.

[*He drops dead*]

MOTHER HEN

He's dead.

What a strange vigil I kept when I found my children

cold with death!

How I watched over them there on the killing fields

when I got up in the frozen morning

and abandoned them there where they'd fallen

to look at the road in front of me.

The path ahead served me as my bandage and my water and my sponge

it soothed my wounds.

The journey continues where it ends I haven't a clue.

I envy men who fall asleep in the homes they grew up in

surrounded by faces they know.

Onwards.

All this mess of human driftwood

is lies and illusion.

Order is the law of the universe making all things whole.

[*She takes off her smock. Sewn all over her dress are hundreds of little cloth bags*]

The ashes from my flock of kids.

O Captain my captain I return them to you.

[*She empties the bags on to the earth, which she rakes with a stick or ISMAIL's Kalashnikov*]

Let's carry on.

Oh oh! Is there anyone still left here?

Oh is there anyone?

Oh someone! Surely there's still someone?

[*With small tired footsteps she heads into the distance*]

FINAL BLACKOUT